BEATING THE
CHURCHGOING
BLAHS

An Adventurer's Guide
to Survival in the Church

ROBERT THORNTON HENDERSON

INTERVARSITY PRESS
DOWNERS GROVE, ILLINOIS 60515

InterVarsity Press is the book-publishing division of Inter-Varsity Christian Fellowship, a student movement active on campus at hundreds of universities, colleges and schools of nursing. For information about local and regional activities, write Public Relations Dept., InterVarsity Christian Fellowship, 6400 Schroeder Rd., P.O. Box 7895, Madison, WI 53707-7895.

Scripture quotations designated RSV are from the Revised Standard Version of the Bible copyrighted 1946, 1952, 1971 by the Division of Christian Education of the National Council of the Churches of Christ in the U.S.A. and are used by permission. All rights reserved. Scripture quotations designated NIV are from the Holy Bible: New International Version. Copyright © 1978 by the New York International Bible Society. Used by permission of Zondervan Bible Publishers.

Distributed in Canada through InterVarsity Press, 860 Denison St., Unit 3, Markham, Ontario L3R 4H1, Canada.

Cover illustration: Dan Pegoda

ISBN 0-87784-516-6

Printed in the United States of America

Library of Congress Cataloging in Publication Data

Henderson, Robert T., 1928-
    Beating the churchgoing blahs.

    Bibliography: p.
    1. Church renewal.   2. Pastoral theology.   I. Title.
BV600.2.H396   1986   253   86-21338
ISBN 0-87784-516-6

19	18	17	16	15	14	13	12	11	10	9	8	7	6	5	4	3
99	98	97	96	95	94	93	92	91	90	89	88	87				

This book is dedicated to my fellow adventurers, my Christian family in the Blacknall Memorial Church of Durham, the Canal Street Church of New Orleans and the First Church of Hendersonville in whose company and with whose patience and prayers I—and we— learned these lessons. But especially it is dedicated to my Betty who has sustained me in prayer in a long and exciting journey which is recorded in these pages.

An Adventurer's Guide to Survival in the Church

Some months ago I was participating in a gathering of evangelical leaders from around the nation. It was an exciting gathering, full of expectation. Here were educators, authors, preaching superstars, outstanding laypersons—in short, a dazzling display of gifted Christian leadership. And then there were the rest of us!

During the early part of this gathering we took time to get acquainted, each of us sharing how God had brought us to this point. We heard amazing accounts of God's faithfulness, thrilling stories of people's spiritual pilgrimages. Some had come to Christ in dramatic ways. Others had been discipled by some of God's great saints. Still others had risen to national prominence in what seemed a story of God's good purpose and providence.

Just before coffee break came my turn to share. I felt a little out of place. Apart from a pair of genuine and consistent Christian parents, there has been nothing glamorous or dramatic about my Christian adventure. To be honest, I had to share my years in the wilderness, in difficult and struggling-for-survival churches, seeking to understand God's design in bringing renewal to such unlikely places. I certainly have many causes to rejoice in God's goodness and faithfulness, but my life in the church has been full of pain, loneliness and impatience, even anxiety.

At the coffee break a gentle and sensitive brother sidled up to me and initiated the whole train of thought that I shall pursue in this book. "Bob," he said, "yours was the really thrilling story of the morning. You are where most Christians are. Very few Christians experience dynamic congregational life or have contact with gifted disciplemakers. Why, sixty per cent of the American people who profess to be 'born again' don't even go to church. You need to tell your story publicly. That's what people need to hear!"

During these passing months I have been reflecting on his comment. Does it ring a bell with you? It does with me. Hearing the accounts of the "success churches" has so often depressed me. Tales of security and fruitfulness and conversion growth make me wonder if I am on the right track.

Oh, I can really praise the Lord for creative and exciting ministries. I can rejoice in charismatic leadership that produces life and blessing. But when nothing appears to be budging where I am and I have no place to escape, what am I to do?

Would it be too awful to conjecture that for every happy, healthy, fulfilling, growing congregation in this fair land, that there are scores of dismal episodes of ecclesiastical boredom, pious status quo and moribund tradition?

Perhaps that's an exaggeration. But when your whole Christian experience has been devoid of any contact with a Christian church that demonstrates the joy of the new creation, then you are sorely tempted to be a bit pessimistic. It doesn't really help a whole lot to read all the volumes on the church, how wonderful it is, and how essential it is to our Christian health. Despite all the books on the theology of the church extolling the wonders of the Christian community (and I have read more than most), again and again I find that very few of the people who come through our congregation's membership class understand the joyous news of Jesus Christ and the purpose of the church as the community of that joyous news. For most of them the church has been an experience of grim resignation, of dismay, of guilt, of friction, of conflict and of perseverence in the rituals.

What a parody! If tens of thousands of people go through the motions and never know the joy of the community in the Holy Spirit, does this really glorify God or exhibit his purpose?

I was talking recently with a friend of mine, a gifted official in his state government. "Look, Bob," he said to me, "all week long I'm dealing with a vast bureaucratic network and all the crises in scores of local governments. And when Sunday comes and I need my batteries recharged so that I can function as God's child in state government, what happens? I teach Sunday school. I'm on the board of elders. They want me to attend endless committee meetings and resolve the crises in the congregation. Sunday becomes one more work day, and the Christian church something I almost dread. Something's wrong. What do I do?"

Then another young friend of mine, a poet and a remarkable lay theologian, told me about moving to a community where the church's biggest enterprise of the year was to gather enough pine needles to mulch down the church's azalea beds. "Bob," she protested, "I don't want to pick up pine needles! I want to be joined to those who have some vision of God's purpose in the world. What do I do? What good is the church?"

Still another friend, chairman of his congregation's witness committee, told me about their church. It hadn't grown in thirty years, nobody ever visited their congregation and, to top things off, the congregation wasn't disturbed by this. How does one carry out any evangelizing work in a congregation of people who are essentially content to go on indifferent to the world outside just as long as there are enough folk left to pay the bills?

I could tell you more unhappy stories like these, but you don't need that. You could tell me your own. But what should we do in such an unhappy situation? What can we do?

Chuck the whole thing?

Accept the church as a respectable social context?

Endure it with resignation?

Get angry?

Feel guilty?

Pray for revival, but remain passive?

Become a church gadfly?

No, we've got to move beyond cynicism and guilt. Let me tell you what I hope to do in this book. I am a fellow adventurer. The ground I am describing is familiar territory. And the reason I write is that I know that there is a way through this dilemma. There is a vast mission field today, that of these everywhere congregations that once were alive and now are in a holding pattern and near death. Yet, somehow in these congregations of every description and Christian tradition the name of Jesus Christ is present, even if only in a misty tradition or in the hymns. And I believe that the God and Father of my Lord Jesus Christ rejoices and is glorified when such congregations begin to awaken and to express again the corporate joy of the new creation in Jesus Christ.

I happen to be an organic gardener. I may also be some kind of a masochist. But I get a lot of joy out of beginning with the impossible soil in my yard and working until it has changed from sterile pipe clay into rich humusy soil with tilth and necessary nutrients to produce rich growth. That transformation is not fortuitous. It develops from the implementation of valid principles of plant growth and soil transformation. Having said that, however, doesn't mean that it is easy or quick. A good, deep, cultivated bed takes at least three years, maybe more.

So also in the transformation of congregations. God has not left us without the clues to spiritual stagnation, nor has he left us without the principles of renewal. I have learned these, and I hasten to add, *am* learning these over thirty years and in three different congregations. I have watched them take effect, and I am still watching them take effect. And I want to share some of my excitement and experience with you.

I have this vision, this dream, of the God of our salvation being glorified in the dreariest and most unlikely congregations as they burst into kingdom life and joy and fruitfulness. But the essential element is for some people to accept this ministry as their calling, to stay there, to accept the pain and the conflict, to be available to the Spirit of God, to be his Shammah until this happens.

And what or who is Shammah? Shammah is the patron saint of congregational renewal! I know because I made him that. You will find him in 2 Samuel 23:11. He was brought to my attention by a missionary to China some years back, and I have identified with Shammah ever since.

> And next to him was Shammah, the son of Agee the Hararite. The Philistines gathered together at Lehi, where there was a plot of ground full of lentils; and the men fled from the Philistines. But he took his stand in the midst of the plot, and defended it, and slew the Philistines; and the LORD wrought a great victory. (RSV)

Any survivor can identify with Shammah. Here he is, sent by his great captain David to this unglamorous plot of lentils, that is, a beanpatch. Everybody who is sent with him splits, goes AWOL, and leaves Shammah there in his loneliness with this intimidating horde of Philistines coming down on him. And with whatever anguish went on inside of him, and whatever unkind thoughts about his fellows (and maybe even David), he did what he had been commanded to do. He had the honor of his great captain in view. Then, because of his faithfulness in what appeared to be an impossible situation, the Scripture records that "the LORD wrought a great victory."

I cannot recount how many times in my adventure, when I despaired of anything ever happening, and when every human factor was discouraging, I would remember that I was there by the design of my Great Captain, who had brought me there in his providence to uphold the honor of his name. I was not always, or even frequently, triumphal about this. I usually would simply say, "O.K., Lord! Shammah checking in here. I don't know what I'm doing here, and I'm not sure I like it, but you are the one who sent me and so here I am, holding on to this plot of lentils. Go to work on me and through me so that the victory will be yours.

Over and out."

Perhaps, then, we could create a new missionary order, "The Order of Shammah," to seek the honor of God's name in the myriad of his congregations where his name and his glory have become little more than a relic. I can get excited about that!

This book then could be entitled "Shammah's Guide to Faithfulness in Beanpatch Churches"—but even that is not enough. What I want to write is a very realistic "Christian's Guide to Joy in the Church." I want to do it with a bit of holy irreverence, with some mirth, much honesty, some redemptive iconoclasm, and hopefully with some good biblical and theological substance. All with a good purpose.

Though a pastor myself, I have laypeople in view primarily because they are the vast majority of God's people.

Isn't this a dangerous task to set ourselves to? Yes! But what a happy vision if we complete the journey!

* * * *

Glory be to the Father, and to the Son, and to
the Holy Spirit. Amen.

* * * *

1
Welcome to Reality

Jonah didn't object to being a prophet, but he certainly wanted to choose the place and the people to whom he was to prophesy! When God landed him in that abominable Nineveh he felt double-crossed. And when God actually brought the city of Nineveh to repentance, Jonah went out and pouted!

I think it was Oswald Chambers who chided us about wanting to set the stage for our own martyrdom. But that is a trap that is easy to fall into. Like "Use me, Lord, but not here. It's not like I imagined it. Why, they don't even sing the hymns that I'm used to, and the people here don't even seem to believe."

Or, "I want to be a part of a real New Testament church!" O.K., do you want the church at Rome with the shadow of an authoritarian government hanging over it and a congregation with tensions between the weak and the strong, the meat-eaters and vegetarians? Or do you prefer the church at Corinth, with sexual aberrations and jealousy over spiritual gifts, as well as other subtle intrusions of the pagan culture? Or perhaps you would like the church at Colossae with a philosophical gnosticism gnawing away at its insides? The church at Galatia was a good New Testament church. All it had was a problem with some Jewish principles added to the message of Jesus Christ that Paul roundly condemns.

But there's no sense playing out this silly argument. The New Testament churches, both in the epistles and in the seven churches of Revelation, are as human as the ones you and I live in. They are riddled with interpersonal conflicts, doctrinal deviations, intrusions of heresies, enculturation by pagan society and involvement in immorality. Occasionally they display significant strengths and commendable faithfulness, but it's always a battle and an uphill trek.

The church between the ages is seldom glamorous, or easy, or clean, or without conflict. And if you think it is, or if you think a particular congregation somewhere has got it all together, you probably ought to be suspicious, because the battle between the aeon of death and the aeon of life never ceases.

A Personal Episode

Let me tell you a personal episode. I had become part of a congregation, early in my adult life, that was really bad—*discouraging* is too mild a description. There had been four pastors in a five-year period, and the remaining faithful members who had any appreciation of the meaning of the Christian message were without much hope. There were all manner of internecine conflicts that made the whole chemistry of the congregation explosive. So here I was! And the temptation came to seek escape. After all, there must be some fine congregation somewhere waiting to be blessed by my presence and gifts!

And in that state of mind the Lord spoke to me in whatever way it is that God communicates unmistakably to his own. And the message was something like this: "O.K., Bobby! Where are you going to go? If you don't believe that I can work here where I have put you, then how can you trust me to work anywhere else? Oh, to be sure, you can probably find a place that is humanly more congenial and pleasant, but how can you believe that I can do my work there if I can't do it here? How do you know I will use you there if I can't use you here? After all, I brought you to this congregation to seek my honor here and my promises are upon you. What happens to my honor if you run to another place? Can you trust me to work here, Bobby?"

Well, that was a heavy confrontation. I can remember the very place where I was praying. God backed me into a corner and put the issue to me. It was an agonizing moment for me. I had been discouraged enough to pray: "Lord, if you want me to stay with this congregation, don't let me get invited (tempted?) to go anywhere else." And now God laid down to me the issue of faith in his ability to bring life and renewal into Nineveh! I had to believe that he *could*, or else just hang it up as far as my faith in God's working anywhere was concerned.

And so I stayed. And God brought me into contact with a few other adventurers in that congregation, and over a period of several years and after many prayers the whole flavor and complexion of that congregation was transformed by God in his faithfulness. He taught us that the principles of renewal are there in Scripture, and when applied with patience, he is pleased to bring new creation into the community. It was not always an easy time. The "prince of darkness grim" doesn't allow salvation to be visited upon a congregation without venting his malice. That's axiomatic! Yet the end result was a congregation that God has been pleased to use fruitfully over many years now. When I visited that family of God some months back after a long absence, I was so moved that I could hardly speak, such was the joy.

We are so like Jonah, aren't we? We're for God and his honor— but not in this Nineveh! "Make me your witness, but deliver me from this unlikely place."

Who's fooling whom? To be faithful to our calling, to be a child of the light, to be a survivalist or a renewalist or a witness in any place or at any time will without exception involve:

pain,
stretching,
discouragement,
weariness,

dismal days,
tears,
loneliness, . . .
. . . and seasons of refreshing from the presence of the Lord,
. . . and the inestimable joy and surprises of his grace.
It is a calling to fill up in our flesh "what is still lacking in regard
to Christ's afflictions, for the sake of his body, which is the
church" (Col 1:24 NIV).

The Church in a Consumer Society

Part of the problem we face, especially in the United States, is our
consumer society. We have been taught to covet what we don't
have, and we have transferred this into our Christian lives so that
we also shop for the church which can do the most for us. Or if
that is not possible, then we read the pop-Christian books which
tell us about such churches, and because we can't have them,
we hunker down and pout that our particular church is not like
that!

We tout the large and successful and innovative and popular
churches, and this, by virtue of the disparity with our own scene,
breeds a subtle or overt discontent. Successful, colorful and growing churches package their programs and write articles about their
ministry and send their pastors off to address large church con-
ferences, with the suggestion that if everyone would buy their
procedures, we would all live happily ever after. This is another
form of our consumer society. Unfortunately the presentations
seldom mention costly obedience, suffering, spiritual conflict, worship, sharing Christ's afflictions for the sake of his body.

I do not at all mean this to sound like sour grapes or jealousy.
But there is often a superficiality in North American church renewal movements that will not stand the searching light of Scripture. There are some idols that are being offered to us that smell
of prestige and wealth and success much more than they savor of
holiness and obedience and a zeal for the name of God and his
kingdom.

Conversion to Reality

The notion of the ideal church, the pure church, the alive church, is the first stage we have to work through in our conversion to reality. It has to do with the *illusion*—the unrealistic human picture of the perfect church, that is, a womb where I am nurtured and blessed, where the faith is pure and my soul is uplifted, where we worship and serve and love and share with one heart and one mind. Ah, blessed illusion!

Don't get me wrong. It is not bad to have dreams. But the idea of church life without pain, struggle and conflict is an unbiblical illusion, a failure to come to grips with the fact that the battle of the ages is being waged in every village, in every generation, in every congregation and every parish.

What kinds of illusions do you come with? What demands do you make on your congregational family? Do you see the church as a grand hotel with doormen and bellmen there to minister to your every need and to relieve all your tensions, with little cards that say, "If you have suggestions for the management which would make your stay with us more pleasant, please write them here and submit them at the desk. We are here to please you."

Or do you expect rhapsodic preaching that simply lifts you out of this world? Or activities to relieve your boredom? I'm not being facetious. A few years ago in the Gallup study on the "Unchurched American" the responses to what would bring unchurched professing Christians back into the church was a catalog of fascinating components such as athletic teams for the family, pastors who were good counselors and the like. All of them were essentially good things, but there was no mention of anything having to do with the kingdom of God, with Jesus Christ and the faith and life that flows from him. As a matter of fact there was a resistance to the church involving itself in anything of social controversy. So much for Jesus and the prophets!

Anyhow, that illusion will last until the second stage of our conversion sets in—namely, *disillusion*. There is a human disillusionment which takes place when you discover or are ambushed by the fact that the congregation in which you are engaged is not glamorous at all. It's the pits! The people in the church are not at all what you expected. Why, some aren't even believers. Some say the most hateful things. The leaders are incompetent. People gossip and couldn't care less about anybody else. They are impervious to change. Some have awful lifestyles or are just plain rakes.

"The Kingdom is in the midst of your enemies," said Martin Luther, "and he who will not suffer this does not want to be of the Kingdom of Christ; he wants to be among friends, to sit among roses and lilies, not with the bad people but the devout people. O you blasphemers and betrayers of Christ! If Christ had done what you are doing who would ever have been spared?"[1]

And because this between-the-ages community always exists in the conflict between darkness and light, I'm not really sure that the disillusioning ever ceases. If nothing else, there is that interminable impatience that afflicts everyone who longs for the fulfillment of the kingdom. We become weary with the slow-paced progress, the baby steps or the backward steps that are and always have been the church's lot.

So what are the disillusioning factors you bring with you? What are the dismaying, discouraging, distracting, demeaning, destructive elements in your sojourn in the church? I use all of those words to remind you that such never come from the Holy Spirit! They are all descriptions of the character of that great archenemy of Christ and his people, and he delights to do all in his power to erode the faith and joy and community of the people of God. It is by that index that I always evaluate the atmosphere (translate that advice, suggestions, criticisms, feelings) of the church.

For instance, there are certain comments that immediately turn on my yellow lights. *What's wrong with this church? I'm not sure that this church is going anywhere. There's no place in this church for me anymore. The pastor and leaders are not listening to the people. I don't like all of these new ideas in our church. These new members are taking over the church. I don't think most of the people here know the Lord. In the church I used to go to we did things differently. This church is dying!*

Look at all the members leaving. We never sing any hymns that I know.

All nice little comments that cast a pall over the conversation and put the blame on someone or something else. And they crop up again and again. I, for one, have been hurt, abandoned, betrayed and discouraged more by my evangelical friends, by my Christian brothers and sisters, than I ever have by non-Christians. I have had more thoughtless wounds inflicted by fellow church members than I can ever imagine by an enemy.

Kefa Sempangi of Uganda in *A Distant Grief* tells of one of his most active elders who betrayed him to the cruel forces of Idi Amin. Should we be surprised? Judas was one of Christ's intimates! Read the stories of twentieth-century martyrs, and not infrequently you will find that they lost their lives through the fearful instrumentality of other Christians. It looks different from the perspective of distance.

Disillusionment can be doctrinal. The church expresses laxity or looseness on some point of Christian belief. Or it can exhibit indifference to some behavioral matter, ethical concern or issue of injustice. It is not difficult to make a case that a goodly part of the North American church is still chained to economic, political and cultural idols.

In this disillusionment the Psalms are a timeless resource. In the Psalms it is not always the pagans, the Canaanites or the ungodly forces outside of Israel that afflict the godly. No, it is the wicked inside the nation who seek to destroy with lying mouths and snares.

If an enemy were insulting me,
    I could endure it;
if a foe were raising himself against me,
    I could hide from him.
But it is you, a man like myself,
    my companion, my close friend,
with whom I once enjoyed sweet fellowship
    as we walked with the throng at the house of God.
(Ps 55:12-14 NIV)

Amid the disillusion the believer, the adventurer, submits himself to the court of God's mercy and grace. And here, away from human view, we can also take vengeance on our adversaries. Does that sound totally impious? I do not make any apologies for the statement. One of the functions of the Psalms is to enable us to vent our human hurt and dismay in the presence of the innumerable company of other saints, and yet all the while to know that God himself hears us in mercy and, in the wonder of his infinite goodness and righteousness, will deal with both us and our adversaries.

Your congregation, the place where you live and struggle at this moment in history, is the book of Revelation in microcosm. It is the same warfare between the Beast and Lamb and the same strengths and weaknesses that have confronted every Christian and Christian community from the beginning.

And here is where most adventurers bail out! Or go out and start another "illusion" congregation! Here is where most visionary church renewalists miss the real joy of Christian community. Here is where we may fail to see the congregation, the church, as a community in process and under grace. It is in this disillusioning moment that we may forget the atonement where a holy God came among sinful humankind and in unimaginable love purchased forgiveness, not because of merit, but because of grace. It is here that the conflict of the ages takes its toll. Those who feel most keenly the preciousness of Christ's body are usually the most easily disheartened when they see its imperfections.

Yet if we are to accomplish anything for Christ's kingdom, we must move into the third stage, namely, that of the *reality* of the church as a community of sinners under grace, as a community of the people of the Lamb of God dwelling in the conflict of the ages, a people needing to be continually evangelized and re-evangelized. Here we must experience Christ in our brothers and sisters, imperfect and fickle though we are.

When we accept this reality and are converted to the ministry of love and prayer and patience and burden-bearing and long-suffering, we become available to Jesus Christ to be his instruments of praise! In this reality the image and character of Christ is forged in our lives by the Holy Spirit. Among real fragile human beings, amid the tragic and flawed present age, the community and the powers of the age to come emerge in new creation.

And this is the beginning of the adventure.

Would that reality would forever dispel illusion and disillusion! But it doesn't. The illusion of the ideal church and the consequent dismaying experience of the disillusioning church keep coming back so that we have to be reminded again and again of the reality which is God's gift to us. This too is part of the adventure.

2
Pioneer Plunge

Thirty miles north of me in the Blue Ridge Mountains is a beautiful conference center called Windy Gap. And a few miles out of the formal conference center is a wilderness area, brute mountainous terrain, which is the site of what are called Pioneer Plunges. A Pioneer Plunge is a venture by the hardy and foolhardy in which they go up into this area and create for themselves the necessities for survival and in the process learn to develop a supportive community. Two realities, then, emerge out of a Pioneer Plunge: a basic civilization and a basic community.

I must confess that there are some churches that present the same sort of challenge, almost daring you to survive. In all too many parishes and assemblies you can find all the ecclesiastical furniture, stained wood pews, red carpet, pulpits and altars and endless church-school classrooms you want, not to mention vested clergy and expected committees, and yet find only dim vestiges of what the Christian church is supposed to be. And though there are people, members, parishioners, even professed believers, in the place of community you find only the brute wilderness of religion. Suspicion, formal and indifferent associations, evangelical amnesia, and other dismaying challenges to your Christian health and survival abound. These churches, to one committed to renewal, are a veritable Pioneer Plunge!

Where to begin? How to survive?

Were I to volunteer for the Pioneer Plunge program at Windy Gap, I'm quite sure I would not just take off thoughtlessly and fortuitously and trust that I might make it. Though some rugged individualists might be up to that, I'm not quite *that* adventuresome. No, I think I would want to sit down with someone who had been there before, say my friend Jim Hornsby who led the plunges there for several years, and find out everything I could about the wilderness there, about the kind of community and survival techniques that had helped others before. I'd want to know exactly what the initiators of the whole program had in mind, what its purpose was in the minds of the founders.

Likewise, as one who senses the nudgings of the Holy Spirit, the call of God to be his agent of awakening and renewal in somnolent if not moribund congregations, then I would by all means want to know something, not only of the history of the church, but of what the initiator, the creator, the Lord of the Church, had in mind for it in the first place. What I'm saying is that it is to our advantage to understand not just the phenomenon of a particular local church, but the theology and history of the whole church of which this particular episode is but a part. Then, in the light of all of that, we might ask what God wants to accomplish through us here in this place and among these people.

If I had that kind of briefing for Windy Gap's Pioneer Plunge, then I would move into the wilderness with at least a vision of what was to transpire in the next days and weeks. I would know some of the booboos that had befallen others before me. And I would have a strategy for doing what the whole Pioneer Plunge program wanted to do and to accomplish. O.K.?

So let's take a quick walk through the purpose and the history of the Christian church so that we can gain perspective on our particular task in whatever our own "little brown church in the vale" or ecclesiastical wilderness happens to look like. All too often the history and theology of the church are a point of weakness among evangelicals, if not missing entirely. The popular evangelical mind puts the focus on the personal experience of Christ, too frequently to the neglect of the experience of the community of faith into which Christ calls us, if Holy Scripture is to be our authority. And if this wholesome understanding of the community of the new creation is obscured in the Christian mind, then not only does a major part of the New Testament become unintelligible, but the gospel of our salvation is severely truncated.

I Will Build My Church

At a critical moment in the lives of the disciples of Jesus, he told them that he was going to build his church and that the gates of death (Hades) would not be able to prevail against it (Mt 16:18). This intriguing prediction came on the heels of Peter's confession that Jesus was indeed the long-awaited Messiah, the Son of the Living God.

What was Jesus saying about the church? And how does it relate to his role as Messiah? What does it have to do with the great salvation he came to accomplish? The Greek word used here is *ekklesia,* which means "assembly" or an "assembly called together for a purpose" or a "called-out people."

Then, though Jesus doesn't use the word significantly again (except in Mt 18:17), he unmistakably teaches his disciples about a community of faith in which they shall live. There is a "one anotherness" about his sense of their future. His salvation is not intelligible in terms of merely private faith and obedience. And as the Holy Spirit comes upon the waiting band of disciples, and as they explode into obedient witness, we see Jesus actively building his church. Multitudes turn in repentance from darkness to light and are baptized publicly and are drawn together in community, in a shared life. In this community they are informed about their new life by the teachings of the apostles. They break bread together. They share their lives and their possessions. There is gladness and singleness of heart. There are crises and Spirit-given solutions. There are challenges and new dimensions of obedience and worship. So a community of worship emerges, a missionary community, a new kind of society with new priorities and with a mysterious power. In fact "the powers of the age to come" (Heb 6:5) rest upon it.

Then the New Testament contains letters addressed to the church, to Christians dwelling together in community. And not a small part of those letters relates to the dynamics of their togetherness, to the disciplines of community, to the demonstrations of love, to the "how to's" of the community of God's new creation.

Early in the church's life there emerged a baptismal creed which affirms belief in the "holy catholic church" and "the communion of the saints" (Apostles' Creed, circa 2nd century). By the fourth century the Nicene Creed affirms belief in the "one holy catholic and apostolic church" as an essential of the Christian faith. By this time these communities of salvation, the new creation in Jesus Christ, were to be found in India, North Africa, Europe and the whole of the Roman world, and who knows where else? Soon they would be in China!

It is impossible to know the exact forms in which these assemblies emerged. Perhaps it is not important. Believers found each other. They met in homes and households. They met in the open air. Sometimes they often met clandestinely and under great danger. They sensed that they were the people of one Lord. But they had differences, and we see them struggling with those conflicts in belief and practice fairly early in their existence.

Only with Constantine's establishing of the Christian faith in the early fourth century do we see any significant development of church buildings in which congregations would meet in larger numbers. Though the distinction between clergy and laity began as early as the second century, only now did the distinction begin to harden. At the beginning all were God's people, the *laos,* and each had gifts. And some of those gifts were pastoral, teaching and apostolic gifts, but they were gifts among equals, among the brothers and sisters of the faith. The emergence of a clergy class changed the complexion of things sizably. It meant that the laity of God were treated as different and often subservient; it meant that the church began to be built around the clergy.

Soon bishops became distinguished from other elders, and those in larger communities became known as "metropolitans." Eventually the bishop of Rome (the Pope) became the leading figure in the Western Church. Similar developments took place also in the Eastern Church and in the Nestorian Church and the Coptic Church, but I will pursue this sketchy history in the West since that is my primary concern.

With the development of a hierarchical kind of church structure, and with the complacency and carelessness that ensued the church's establishment by Emperor Constantine, it didn't take long for all kinds of erosions of faith, life, and sense of calling and uniqueness to manifest themselves in the church. Some handled this by isolating themselves from the church as community and giving themselves to devotion and prayer in solitary places such as the desert. Isolation still appears as an attractive option for some, but it deprives the practitioner of the redeeming disciplines of the community of faith.

By the late fifth century, and in protest of the laxness within the church, Benedict of Nursia went apart to pray and fast. In a grotto in Subiaco, Italy, about A.D. 500 his vision of the Lord led him to initiate a new form of church life and renewal with the formation of the first monastic order. His *Rule of St. Benedict* is a classic study of communal discipline in its most redemptive sense of a life together in subjection to one another in order to produce a context of devotion to Jesus Christ.

In the millennium which transpired between St. Benedict and the dawn of the Protestant reformation, the church was, of course, the Church of Rome, though we should make mention of the split with the Eastern Orthodox Church in A.D. 1054. There was good leadership and corrupt. The form of the church was primarily that of a congregation gathering in a consecrated building with a priest celebrating the Eucharist or Mass, with few indeed who understood the apostolic teachings or the purpose of the "called out people of God" as a part of God's plan for the ages. The protests and renewal movements, if one may generalize, were found in the monastic orders and in occasional reformers, who tended to become the object of the church's scorn and were usually executed. Among these were some of the church's great figures: Marsiglio of Padua, Savonarola, John Hus, John Wycliffe and others. Yet that stream of apostolic proclamation continued to emerge periodically and had an impact on the church.

Other figures in this millennium were effective in other ways. We cannot overlook the colorful Francis of Assisi, whose uninhibited acceptance of the teachings of the Sermon on the Mount perplexed and challenged the church in the thirteenth century, and still do today. The monastic orders of both men and women that grew up around his high-spirited example were a breath of life in an arid period.

Because history is mostly silent, it is difficult to know what other forms of community might have been present. Undoubtedly there were multitudes of believing folk who met together apart from the formal structures to share their faith in Jesus Christ, their prayers and their lives. The great creator of the church has a way of drawing together those in whose lives he is at work.

But let me hasten on. The event which we call the Protestant Reformation was an event of renewal in the holy catholic church. The emerging new traditions were attempts to reclaim the apostolic teachings and to form, or reform, the church in the light of those teachings. What we now call "denominations" are for the most part renewal movements which took on institutional form. Luther discovered faith and grace and the finished work of Christ as he studied Scripture. The Roman Church rejected his protests, and there emerged a church around Luther which we call (what else?) the Lutheran Church. John Calvin, in his study of Scripture, sensed there the glory and the majesty of the sovereign God who was working out his purpose in Jesus Christ. The Roman Church saw him as a threat, and around him grew up the Reformed

Churches. Menno Simmons felt the other reformers were too comfortable with this present age of darkness, and from his teachings came the Anabaptist and Mennonite traditions.

These protesting and renewing movements precipitated in the Roman Church a reappraisal of their own teachings known as the Counter Reformation. With the definitions of doctrine affirmed by the Council of Trent (1562-63) the Roman Church girded itself to cope with the Protestant movement. Rather than bringing unity, it seemed to harden the Roman Church and the Protestant movement into warring camps.

With the liberating effect of the Protestant movement, there began to spring up all kinds of Christian churches, movements and assemblies. One of the scandals of the history of the Christian church, however, is the bloodshed that went along with this. Albeit, if you can look at it historically, you see the Lord of the church in the ebbs and flows of history building his church.

In 1722 a group of exiles out of central Europe gathered on the estate of a German nobleman, Count Nikolaus von Zinzendorf, and as they gave themselves to worship and prayer an awakening to fresh life, power and obedience to Jesus Christ took place. The result was a missionary movement out into the regions where the name of Jesus was not known. These Moravians, aliens and exiles that they were, became the harbingers of a new missionary outreach.

The liberating effect of the Protestant movement, also, made possible the proliferation of an unimaginable diversity of new church expressions. Some were theological in their origins, that is, reactions to the theological excesses or deficiencies of the Roman Church. Some were evangelistic movements which took on institutional form; for example, the Methodist movement under Wesley. To be candid, some were nothing more than separatist movements of Christians who were like obstreperous siblings who simply couldn't get along with others in the family. Yet, whatever the origin, and whatever the ecclesiastical and theological shortcomings we may detect, we can see the leavening effect of the

Christian faith moving across the face of the earth. Jesus Christ is building his church!

Some of these traditions are quite easily traced. Their history is clearly written. Others are not. With the development of English congregationalism, for example, there arises quite visibly (though that kind of thing was not all that new) an independent church stream in which a group of Christians may gather and have no formal tie to other churches, except by voluntary associations. This phenomenon is abundantly evident in the twentieth century as one seeks to trace the ecclesiastical roots of many Baptist traditions as well as independent and Bible churches. This form of the church has moved into many nations with the missionaries of the independent and free church traditions.

In the twentieth century a new phenomenon has arisen—pentecostalism—which is by any measurement one of the fastest growing influences in the Christian world. Not only has it produced its own denominational structures, but has markedly influenced many, if not most, of the other ecclesiastical traditions.

All of this is to say that one must be most magnanimous in dealing with the Christian church in all of its expressions. It is a history of faithfulness and decline, faith and unbelief, revival and apostasy—and yet in the mystery of God's good purpose in Jesus Christ, a church which all of the power of death and hell cannot withstand. Just the moment one tradition, in its vigor and pride, writes off another as unworthy or dead or apostate, then you can almost count on it: God surprises everybody with a breath of new life and power, and out of the rubble arises, phoenixlike, a new witness to the faith of Jesus Christ.

In 1975, I was, with twenty-eight evangelical Protestants, a guest of the Curia of the Roman Church. Now I am a born and bred Protestant, so you can imagine some of my misgivings at being on the inside of the Roman Church system for that two-week period. It was there that an awakening took place in me. I was not face to face with an impersonal ecclesiastical form, but with real persons who were also believers in Jesus Christ, who loved and served him, who were baptized into his name, and in accordance with their tradition were living out that devotion. I found ordained persons teaching "Reformation doctrines" in the seminaries of the Roman Church. I found Catholic charismatics gathered in Bible study, singing Scripture songs, praying in tongues and seeking to evangelize those outside the church. What hath God wrought? As a card-carrying Protestant, I find dimensions of the teachings of the Roman Church that just don't compute. But here I was experiencing genuine trust in the gospel of the kingdom of God as taught by our Lord Jesus Christ.

The church is often a parody, frequently an enigma, if not a contradiction and a downright scandal. So, what's new? One has only to read the letters to the seven churches in the early part of the Revelation to John to see that this was also true at the end of the first century. So it has been ever since. Yet somehow this is all part of God's purpose in joy—the continual struggle of the church as the community of light living in the midst of the aeon of darkness.

In the rich tapestry of this history of Jesus Christ building his church, the Christian person doing the Pioneer Plunge in any particular congregation needs to see that same congregation as one tiny element in God's design.

The Clash of Kingdoms

In addition to our having an understanding of the history of the church, it also helps to realize that the church is called to battle against the alien kingdom of darkness.

It has become common to see the church as living "between the ages." The idea is displayed graphically in figure 1. The parabola that opens out to the left represents the kingdom of darkness or of Satan—this present evil age. It is that fallen creation with all of the alienation, rebellion, error and cultural darkness that the Scriptures define so thoroughly. Into the midst of this kingdom of darkness Jesus came preaching a new dominion, the kingdom of God. And by his life, atoning death on the cross, and resurrection Jesus inaugurated the kingdom of light or of God—the age to come—which is represented by the other parabola that opens out to the right.

The historical invasion of the Son of God into the realities of the kingdom of darkness and death, that is, his first coming, is the point at which this second parabola has its fixed point. Jesus was quite clear that at a future date he will return and at that return the kingdom of darkness, the aeon of death, will come to an end and his dominion will be consummated.

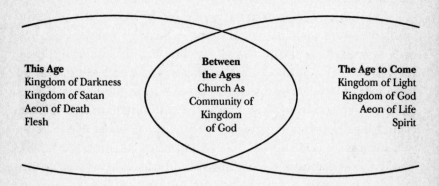

This Age
Kingdom of Darkness
Kingdom of Satan
Aeon of Death
Flesh

Between the Ages
Church As
Community of
Kingdom
of God

The Age to Come
Kingdom of Light
Kingdom of God
Aeon of Life
Spirit

The overlap between the two parabolas represents the era in which we live "between the ages." Here the church is the community of the new creation, the dwelling place of God by the Holy Spirit. But it continues to live in the context of a very vigorous and pervasive aeon of death. What this "between the ages" existence means is that we constantly face the danger of becoming captive to the cultural darkness or to being eroded by the economic and political forces of this present age. The ideologies of every generation tend to infiltrate the community of God's people. The principalities and powers of this age have always sought to co-opt and diminish the church.

Too often the church loses its way and forgets its calling and its message. One of the great ironies of modern history is that Karl Marx was offended by "Christian" industrialists who among oth-

ers exploited poor laborers and children. These Christian industrialists had become blind to some significant dimensions of the
gospel; otherwise they were good, pious church folk. But look
what that partial blindness unleashed in anger against the community of the kingdom of God.

Plunge In

This, then, is the context of the church, and of your particular
church, your Pioneer Plunge. In the midst of all of the joys and
discouragements, the claims and counterclaims, the denominational pluses and minuses, contemporary models and ecclesiastical fads, we need to understand God's purpose for the church. We
need a sense of history, a sense of calling, a sense of the "power
at work" (Eph 3:20) which is able to accomplish immeasurably
more than we can imagine to glorify God in his church. Then
when we set our hand to be a modest agent of God to rebuild, to
restore, to renew his church, we will know that the Risen Lord
who walks among the golden lampstands (Rev 1) walks in the
midst of his church, rejoices over us, and is with us, because we
are part of his good purpose to build his church!

And that is *some* calling!

3
The Church— Who Needs It?

Now wait just a minute, Bob! Give me a break! You're talking about the church as the community of the gospel, of the joyous news of Jesus, out of one side of your mouth and about pain and disillusionment and suffering out of the other. What rubbish! Why all this? I didn't bargain for all the hassle. Who needs the church?"

The answer is, you do. You *really* do. And you *did* bargain for the hassle when you came to Christ.

You came to Jesus, and you came because he called you. And Jesus came to create a new society, a new people, a redeemed community called the church.

You wanted to be delivered from sin, didn't you? You wanted to be forgiven, set free and made new, didn't you? Then you have to understand that there is a whole display of interpersonal evil and societal sin that produces strife, envy, jealousy, party spirit, hatred, dissensions, and such (compare Gal 5:19-21). And we are called to join the battle against these evils. When God the Father adopts us into his family through faith in Jesus Christ his Son, he does not call us into a private and insular experience. Rather, he brings us into his new community where we are taught to live in the Spirit, in the newness of the age to come. He calls us into his family to live among, minister to, grow in the context of other siblings who share our imperfections.

And just as physical growth requires exercise which brings muscular pain and stretching, so there is pain and stretching required to produce growth in redemptive and reconciling relationships within the family of God. The community of salvation needs the disciplines of self-giving love, peaceableness, forgiveness, mutual confession of failure and need, burden-bearing, patience, long-suffering and sharing of possessions as well as singing to one another, sharing life under the word of Christ and serving one another.

These are all New Testament disciplines. And all of these New Testament disciplines say something which needs to be shouted here. They say that we need one another in the body of Christ. These are not disciplines that can be exercised alone. They also remind us that the family of God is made up of persons who make demands upon us. And they say worlds about the stresses and dynamics of the Christian community, if you care to stop to ponder them. For example, if there were no one around to tax your patience, why would you need patience?

These demands of community in the Spirit also expose in us a pernicious self-life that yearns for the blessings of the new creation without the death, without the cross, without the call to servanthood that the kingdom of God requires.

But It's a Long, Long Way from There to Here

From that lofty New Testament conception of the community of the new creation to where most of us live is indeed a difficult transition to make.

Let me tell you about Chris, a German physicist who came to Christ in a weekend conference of evangelical students in Germany. His conversion was no doubt genuine, but his growth derived primarily from small, student-led Bible studies and his own personal reading. His concept of the church reflected two warring notions—one an idealized portrait from his reading of the New Testament, the other his biased understanding of the state church in Germany into which he had been baptized, but which he felt had betrayed him in not bringing him to the knowledge of Jesus. So for several years he had no relationship with any church, believing that the church had become the enemy of the true Christian faith. So, when he landed in our community and was invited to our congregation by the evangelical students at our neighborhood university, he brought with him all of these built-in misgivings.

It was a crack-up! Every Sunday he met me at the church door and harangued me with all of the imperfections of the congregation and all of the things that he felt the New Testament required of the church that he didn't see. And of course he was right There were many things that were absent that all of us desired to be present. He was dealing with the illusion, which we discussed in chapter two.

What got to him was a crisis in his life when his child became critically ill. The love and resources of that imperfect community of Christians surrounded him and his family and brought him through and into an appreciation of the community of Christian pilgrim-adventurers. His eyes were opened to a new and realistic appreciation of how God uses imperfect communities to be communities of grace and love. He subsequently became an elder in the church and made an enormous contribution to the creation of an even more beautiful and biblical expression in the fellowship.

The church frequently and tragically drifts away from its calling to be the vessel of the gospel, but God rejoices to call it back. And Chris helped us with that.

Let me give you another illustration. As I have mentioned already, I enjoy organic gardening. Over the years I have developed a few French-cultivated beds (beds cultivated two- or three-feet deep), and I've worked to get the soil fairly well balanced. I was so proud one winter when I got back the lab report that my soil was near perfect! And as long as I keep working on it, dealing with the soil and discouraging all of the insects which rejoice over all the succulent banquets I provide for them, I come up with a near approximation of what I dreamed.

But, if I ignore that care for a month, I get an infestation of weeds, insects and diseases that visibly mar the image. And if I were to ignore a bed for a year or more, I would find little oak trees, morning glory vines and poison oak, alien grasses and blights of every variety choking out what was once a thing of beauteous delight. The original plants mights still be there, but they would be in serious danger. Any gardener hoping to restore such a bed must begin little by little to engage the disciplines that only with time will return the garden to its intended purpose.

So with the church. When it forgets its message, its Lord, its calling and becomes merely a religious institution with holy water on unholy lives, ritual, priestly hirelings and demanding parishioners, then it hardly looks like a fountain of living waters or the community of Jesus.

One of the effects of such a drift is that Christian people create for themselves a version of the faith that simply filters out the whole communal dimension of the gospel and substitutes a truncated, privatized version. This, of course, is reinforced by a whole culture obsessed with individualism and one's own rights.

The result is to reduce the Christian faith to exclusively personal terms: my forgiveness, my new birth, my inner peace, and how the Sermon on the Mount brings me inner fulfillment. We then studiously avoid the great biblical themes of the church, a holy nation, the family of God, the body of Christ and the communion in the Holy Spirit, among others.

When the Gallup organization did their 1978 study on "The Unchurched American," they discovered that millions of professing Christians and persons who acknowledged a life transforming experience with Jesus Christ seldom if ever attend church gatherings. I have also heard about hundreds of "Spirit-filled" Christians in a small town who don't belong to any church!

What does this say?

It says that we need to address the crucial question of the *why* of the Christian community. And when that is done, we need to address the question of the *how* to restore it where we live and worship and minister.

Why the Church?

Why the church? What purpose does it play in God's purpose of salvation? Why this corporate dimension of Christian faith and life?

It is astonishing to me that so many "disciplemaking courses" leave out this whole subject. They rightfully emphasize Bible study, prayer, obedience, faith-sharing and Christian living, and yet remain completely silent on the disciplines of the Christian community.

Yet Jesus said:

A new command I give you: Love one another. As I have loved you, so you must love one another. All men will know that you are my disciples if you love one another. (Jn 13:34-35 NIV)

I remember once hearing an outstanding evangelical Bible teacher do a whole series of expositions on the letter to the Ephesians without ever mentioning the church. Here is this awesome statement of the mystery of God's will—to bring all things together under one head, even Christ. Here is this declaration of the body of Christ being the fullness of him who fills everything, of the church being the dwellingplace of God by the Holy Spirit. Here is the reminder that the walls of hostility have been brought down in Christ so that there is reconciliation between alienated groups. It is breathtaking. Yet this teacher taught about our individual walk with Christ in the heavenly places. He taught about our deliverance from spiritual death, about spiritual warfare and the whole armor of God—all good teaching—but somehow filtered out the message at the heart of the letter about our life together.

When such an individualized understanding of the church has been our diet, we have little reserve to overcome disillusionment or burnout. When the church seems to be an anachronism or irrelevant, we lack the conviction that the church is necessary to God's plan of salvation. Then we feel we can set it aside without any essential diminishing of our faith or walk with God.

Why then the church?

First, the church is where societal decay, the ravages of sin on the human community, is reversed or redeemed. The church is the community of reconciliation, the paradigm community of the kingdom of God. The church demonstrates the new humanity in Christ and provides evidence of his reconciling work. The church is that mysterious, enigmatic, human-but-not-merely-human community of the new creation which is the dwellingplace of God by the Holy Spirit (Eph 2:22). It is the arena in which we are being recreated into Christ's likeness, and through which his salvation is being modeled and mediated in the world. Always in process and never perfect, the church nevertheless is the central arena of God's activity in the world.

To try to live our new life in Christ apart from the Christian community leaves us incomplete, if not crippled. It is to be orphaned, to be a child without a family.

Part of the mystery of this family experience is that through the pain, through the illusion-disillusion-reality experience, we enter into true freedom and joy and the fulfillment of the new creation! Or, to put it another way, only through the death of my individualism comes the true joy of the communion of the saints. Only by death to my demanding self-life do I discover the redemptive support community for my pilgrimage through this present age.

Having said this much this strongly, I don't want to absolutize this community dimension of the Christian faith. There is an alone dimension as well, but our individual dealings with God and our dealings together in the community of faith are symbiotic. One is incomplete without the other.[1]

The Arena of Discipleship and Sanctification
Another dimension of the *why* of the church has to do with life

and growth and refining as God's children. In the New Testament such growth is seen to take place primarily in the community of salvation, the church. This, of course, is the message of the New Testament letters.

There are several words that figure prominently in the growth disciplines of the New Testament. Jesus told his own disciples to "go and make disciples" so that the concept of *discipleship/disciple-making* is one of those words. Jesus had called the Twelve to come be with him. He lived with them, taught them, listened to them, took them with him, let them get close and ask questions, dealt with their sibling rivalries, sent them out on missions, called them back, rebuked and encouraged them—in short, he reproduced himself in them so that when he was gone they, by the Holy Spirit's empowering, were able to take on the task of seeing Christ formed in others by the same disciplemaking process which Jesus had used with them.

We see this quite clearly in the Acts accounts. Right after Pentecost the believers gathered about the apostles. They learned to live Christ in the midst of a hostile environment, to share their lives, to pray, to preach, to obey, to deal with crises in the community, and to become that community of salvation that Jesus had purposed.

Paul too was a disciplemaker. "Be imitators of me," he said, "as I am of Christ" (1 Cor 11:1 RSV). To the Philippians he wrote, "Whatever you have learned or received or heard from me, or seen in me—put it into practice. And the God of peace will be with you" (Phil 4:9 NIV).

What is apparent is that to be a disciple, or to be "in Christ" (which appears to be Paul's way of expressing discipleship) is always in the context of other Christian sisters and brothers.

If discipleship is to have Christ formed in us, then another important word is *sanctification,* whose root is the word *holy.* And being holy, or being sanctified, as alien as that sounds to modern ears, is always a goal of New Testament Christians.

Sanctification is a good word. It is both a gift given us in Christ

(1 Cor 1:30) and the process of (Eph 5:26; 1 Thess 5:23) making us genuine, of giving us integrity of relationship with the will and character of God. To be holy is to be in a transforming relationship with the living God. Here too we see that the church is holy and that sanctification is always defined in the arena of the church.

Not that God does not, or cannot, graciously do a transforming work in us in solitude. To be sure, the desert fathers found an unusual degree of relationship with God in the mystery of their isolation from all human contacts. But that is not the norm. Every member of the body, in Paul's metaphor of the organism, is intimately connected to and ministering to the life and well-being of the others.

And what is our ultimate goal? To be conformed to the image of Jesus Christ. And what is he like?

Take even a cursory glance at the New Testament documents, and it will strike you that Jesus came as the firstfruits of a whole new kind of humanity. He came as a servant, and he taught that whoever would be great in his new dominion would be the servant of all. He came accepting the agony of the cross for the joy that was before him, and he told those who would follow him that they also must deny themselves and take up their cross and follow him. He announced that to follow him would cause divisions and pain, but that in the midst of all that he would give to his followers a peace unlike anything the world would give, or could give.

He went about doing good, healing the sick, cleansing lepers, feeding the hungry and announcing good news to the poor. Then he told his followers that this same agenda would be the basis for rewards at the end of the age, that their response to the hungry, thirsty, naked, sick and imprisoned would be a response to him.

He gave them a command to love each other as he had loved them. He was shocking in his insistence that he didn't come to bring salvation to the "righteous" but to seek and to save the lost. He modeled the beatitudes which he gave to his followers as the way into blessedness. Paul would later say that the image of Christ being formed in us is that of being like Christ in knowledge, true righteousness, and holiness (Eph 4:24; Col 3:10).

Yet Jesus' call was not simply to individual repentance and faith. The whole basis of his call was that a new reality had intruded itself into our midst, that is, that the kingdom of God had drawn nigh. Repentance and faith then are our response to what God is doing. What will one day be manifest throughout all creation is now to be progressively visible in the present age through the church. The church, the called out people of Jesus Christ, is the community of the kingdom of God.

God's intent was that Jesus be the firstborn among many brethren, that he be the firstfruits of a new creation. The clear implication is that there be a lot more brothers and sisters, much more fruit, which would constitute a new creation, a new race, a new humanity. And that new community would testify to the reality of the dominion of God now present, which was inaugurated by Jesus Christ.

"I will build my church" means that the primary agenda between Christ's first and second coming is the building of his church. That is why the church has always understood the primary work of the Holy Spirit as the creation of the church. If then we are Jesus' disciples, if we have come to him, if we are indwelt by his Spirit of holiness, then concern for the building and welfare of his church must become ours.

Then it is no overstatement when Paul calls the church *the body of Christ*. Somehow, that weird bunch of semipagans in Corinth who had come into contact with Christ were the church, called, of all things, *saints*. These human beings were in the throes of that mysterious alchemy of the Holy Spirit whereby they were being transformed from children of darkness into children of light; they were being recreated after the image of him who had called them.

And why does Jesus work this way? As a demonstration of God's grace. He did what he did as the key figure in the Father's plan for the ages. In horribly imperfect settings, through fickle human beings surrounded by immorality, heresy, ideologies, bad examples and other assorted destructive forces, the body of Christ stands forth as a sign of the kingdom of God and his righteousness.

Thus the joyous news of Jesus and the ever-present hassle of the church are all part of our calling and will be until Christ returns.

The *how* of Christian community is the subject of the rest of this book. The key to joy amid the hassle has to do with the decision which we make to be Christ's disciples, his coworkers in the task of building the church, his dynamic components in conducting his life and power into congregations in which we find ourselves. That decision has to be settled before we go further.

But there may be one thing more. How do we select a church?

How to Select a Church

Do you have a choice of churches? If you are by heritage or local circumstances locked into one particular congregation or tradition, then the question is moot. But if you are looking around and the choice is among several traditional and nontraditional, denominational or independent, Catholic, Protestant, or Pentecostal churches, then there are several things that you ought to keep in mind:

1. The church is more than the local congregation. The confessions of the early church affirmed belief in "one holy catholic and apostolic church." That is to say that no particular congregation or denomination or tradition has a corner on the church. Nevertheless, look for the essentials: (a) belief in the triune God, Father, Son and Holy Spirit; (b) belief in the full deity and humanity of Jesus Christ; (c) belief in the sufficiency and authority of Scripture as the trustworthy source of apostolic faith and (d) an understanding that the church is somehow the community of those who affirm the first three essentials. And you will find to varying degrees that nearly all Protestant, Catholic, Pentecostal, Orthodox, and Independent traditions hold these essentials. Yet a Christian adventurer needs always to be aware that there are

particular congregations that have become inimical to these essentials. There is a pathology of indifference to scriptural doctrines that actually produces a resistance, if not outright hostility, to the clearly stated evangelical truths of the New Testament. Such destructive environments are best avoided. Happily, there are not many of these, but there are some.

2. The church should "walk its talk." That is to say, just because a church makes a big fuss over its evangelical orthodoxy doesn't necessarily mean a lot unless it lives out that orthodoxy in love, obedience, worship and compassion. Conversely, there are times when a church has a very inadequate creedal statement, yet is bearing the fruits of repentance in such a way that the kingdom reality is manifest in that congregation. Appellations such as liberal, fundamentalist, apostate, evangelical are easy to hang on a church, but frequently misrepresent what God is doing or wants to do among the folk of that community.

3. Be aware of your own prejudices and traditions. Just because you have been accustomed to the Baptist tradition doesn't mean that the Lutheran tradition is not viable. We tend to think in terms of the tradition in which we came to Christ or in which we grew up. But the Christian church is rich in diversity. I happen to be a Presbyterian, but in my lifetime I have shared incredible and often surprising experiences of worship and witness with Roman Catholics and Pentecostals and Plymouth Brethren and many others. Choosing, then, may involve other traditions than I am accustomed to.

4. No tradition is complete and perfect. Christ's people probably most often find their nurture in such incomplete settings. I sat one afternoon with British scholar Norman Anderson. He is an evangelical Anglican. It was a time when some Anglican bishops had made some atrociously agnostic statements on major biblical truths. I asked Dr. Anderson how he justified being in the Church of England under such leadership. His response was both abrupt and thrilling. He said: "I am blessed in my own parish. It is there that I find nurture and support. And the Thirty-Nine Articles of

Religion of the Church of England is an evangelical creed. I am not about to forsake my church *because of* or *to* such rascals as those bishops!" Such parallels can be found in every one of the Christian communions.

5. The presence of one disciple in a congregation gives the Lord of the church a vessel of his renewing grace in that congregation.

6. If you believe that the Lord of the church wills to refresh and renew *all* of his church, then you can know that even though your choice is imperfect, God can make you an instrument of his reviving grace in the most unlikely spot.

The flip side of the question about selecting a church is the more painful question, Should I ever leave a church? To that I hasten to answer that as a general rule I'd say no. When all the disciples, who are the "good vitamins," leave a congregation, then the "bad vitamins," or the wolves, or whoever, have a field day, and the honor of God in that congregation is diminished. Richard Lovelace has documented how detrimental the "delta effect" has been when living evangelical forces separate themselves from traditions and congregations in a search for a more pure expression.[2]

At the same time, God does not choose to destroy his own and if a congregation is destroying you and you are not capable of surviving in that context, then choose a more wholesome option if one is available. We need to look carefully at our motives here, however. We have a proclivity to dodge discomfort or to avoid spiritual conflict into which our great Captain has called us, thus going AWOL in the battle for renewal in the church. Even one person can be God's conductor of the life and power of the gospel into a moribund and straying church.

All the same, I must admit that there are unquestionably those situations in which survival is unlikely. Going it alone in a spiritally arid congregation is especially difficult. If you can find someone else in such a congregation then there is support for prayer and encouragement. But that one other is often difficult to find

What does one do? I know of some who survived on the liturgy of some of the more traditional churches, liturgies that are often rich in truth, even though nothing else in the church is. I have known others who for periods simply set apart Sundays as a time of rich and calculated family worship in their homes, yet kept longing and looking for a larger congregation. Just remember in the midst of these distressing situations, that the church is still the Lord's, and that he is with you in your quest, and that though for the moment you are chagrined by the absence of a viable congregation, you still have the responsibility to pray for the church and to seek its welfare where you live.

Thrice blessed are those who have accepted this calling to the battle for the honor of God in his church as God's gift to them— and have stayed and worked and loved and served and prayed— and have seen the faithfulness of God as the rivers of living water began to flow again in the dry riverbeds of an apparently hopeless wilderness.

Some Beginning Rules

And, having accepted such a call, where should you begin?

1. *Rejoice* that God has put you where you are to make you a channel of renewal, to be his gift to that church, even if it seems asleep. Thank God that you're there!

2. *Affirm* everything you can in that church. Be generous in your appraisal. Reach back into its history if you have to. Be positive. There are always some positive factors and dynamics and persons (though often quiescent and obscure) in the most unlikely congregations.

3. *Don't go gadflying* around, comparing your church unfavorably with others.

4. *Don't undermine* your pastor and leadership team. Rather, minister to them (and not condescendingly) as a ministry given to you by the Lord as a sacred stewardship!

5. *Accept the servant role!* With joy do the foot washing. How very much the ministry of the renewal of Christ's church needs the foot

washers, the gentle servants.

6. *Keep yourself alive and healthy.* Maintain the disciplines of spiritual formation and discipleship (see the next chapter).

7. *Practice love,* genuine love (if you are resentful or a prima donna or negative or demanding, it will show). Let that love come forth as gentle evangelism as you let your warm and loving devotion to Christ "slosh over" on others. Let that love share good literature with others as you offer out of your library those good things that will encourage them toward Christ. Let your love be expectant and anticipatory of God's good purpose toward his church. And let your love show in your faithfulness so that when you accept responsibilities, you are dependable and loyal.

8. *Be patient!* This can be a lifetime calling.

9. And patiently, but insistently *pray for seasons of renewal and refreshment* from the presence of the Lord.[3]

Welcome to the Adventure of the Church

What gives the church the sense of adventure is the reminder that in the Fall of humankind in the Garden of Eden, all the fabric of God's purpose for shalom, for harmonious community, was violated, and alienation became the eroding force in human society. In the Second Adam, Jesus, God reveals his purpose to create a new humanity in which there is reconciliation and love and redemption—a church, if you will. And to this new community, in all of its imperfect and in-process manifestations, we are called.

> I urge you to live a life worthy of the calling you have received. Be completely humble and gentle; be patient, bearing with one another in love. Make every effort to keep the unity of the Spirit through the bond of peace. There is one body and one Spirit— just as you were called to one hope when you were called. (Eph 4:1-4 NIV)

You can avoid the church. Many do. But to their own detriment. It is the dwellingplace of God by the Spirit (Eph 2:22). It is the new humanity in Christ (Col 3:12). It is the recipient of his power at work to do more than we ask or think with the purpose of glorifying himself (Eph 3:20-21). It is the participation in Christ Jesus, who for the joy that was set before him endured the cross (Heb 12:2).

So, in some strange and mysterious way, in the depths of God's providence, the church becomes the essential context for sanctification and disciplemaking and for fellowship with Jesus.

And in that mystery Jesus has given us a rite, a sacrament if you will, to remind us of the mystery of his redeeming love and of his church. He said, "Do this when you come *together.*" Yes, "when you are together, . . . my body, my blood of the covenant, take eat, drink of it, . . . as often as you do this you show forth the Lord's death until he comes." The focus is on Christ, but the context is that of the community of faith. Somehow that table of thanksgiving, that Eucharist, is incomplete without others to share in it.

And I doubt if it is even possible to calculate what a critical factor this Eucharist is in producing disciples and saints over all of these intervening centuries. When the tide of evangelical expression was ever so low and the church's priests and ministers were perhaps ever so careless, yet at the table ordinary and imperfect adventurers, such as you and I, met Jesus Christ afresh and were evangelized anew and saw their calling to live Christ with clearer eyes and with hearts made strong.

So let me welcome you anew to the church, to the mystery and the enigma, to adventure and suffering, to the inexpressible joy and wonder of sanctification and discipleship, to the table of thanksgiving, and so to Jesus Christ and his calling to us to be Spirit-filled agents of his new community of the kingdom of God.

4
Do-It-Yourself Disciplemaking

I could tell I was in for it. She was a very attractive and determined-looking person, and she had me fixed in her sights. I had just finished talking about the necessity of the church with a group at a weekend conference, and it was coffee-break time. Here it came: "Yes, all very convincing. Church, discipleship, and all of that. Nice idea! It sounds super *in theory,* Bob. But my question is one of either self-pity or enlightened self-interest—I don't know which. I'm part of the desolation of our church. I'm frustrated and burned out trying to cope with a church which demands of me but never ministers to me.

"How do I keep myself alive and healthy? How do I become mature and fruitful so as to become a part of the answer? It is not as though I had nothing to occupy my time. I have a husband, children who have too much energy, and a full-time profession myself. My husband also is a professional person with a very challenging research project, and he has us. How do I, how do we prosper, become fruitful disciples given the constraints that are upon us? Answer me that!"

So there it was. The question is, How do you become a fruitful disciple if you have no disciplemaker? How do you equip yourself to be a conductor of the renewing life of God into your congregation when the congregation appears to offer you no resources for growth?

I don't have any easy answers, because there aren't any. And the problem runs deep.

I was counseling a despairing theological seminary student one day. He was about to graduate and become a pastor, and he felt that he had no idea what he really wanted to accomplish, or what pastoral ministry would actually be. I believe that good disciplemaking is a teach-coach-model kind of ministry, so I asked him who his models were. He had none. He had come to faith in Christ in a campus evangelistic ministry, but that was about it. Though he and I had only a very casual friendship, I found that he was looking to me as his "long-distance" disciplemaker.

Betty, my wife, was sitting within earshot, and when we were on the way home from the seminary, she began to probe me with my own questions. She asked me who my models were. As I reached back to try to retrieve an answer to that I realized that most of my models were negative ones, people and practices that I definitely did *not* want to be like. We got some good chuckles thinking about that. A lot of my own discipling was "long distance"—seeing or hearing or reading something from afar that prodded me on into maturity in the likeness of Christ.

But, then, that pushed me to another disturbing observation. In the New Testament, the pastor-teacher seems to be the primary focus of disciplemaking in the congregation. He or she is the one (Eph 4:11-12) who is to equip God's people for ministry, until all become mature in the likeness of Christ. Yet, one of the puzzlements of the whole church system is that so very, very few of our seminaries or training schools even touch the disciplines of disciplemaking. One of the consequences of this, in my own experience, is that very few pastors have been discipled themselves or know how to make disciples of others!

This offers some very exciting possibilities. What it means is that there are possibly a whole lot of pastors who need to have the same kind of growth experience you are looking for yourself. They have been endowed in seminary with a whole lot of left-brain knowledge of biblical tools, history and doctrine, but have never been brought to the wholesome and healthy and contagious kind of faith that lets another get close in the dialogical and practical relationship that produces true disciples.

So it may be that your pastor will enter into a mutual kind of disciplemaking experience.

This is partially what got my attention. In one of the wild episodes of my career, I had gone to Berkeley, California, at the height of the Jesus Revolution to be part of a workshop on "Radical Street Christianity." One of my young adult friends had accompanied me. He was a restless, hungry, adventuresome young Christian, and a very productive salesman for a major corporation. During those two weeks in Berkeley we participated in all kinds of open-air Bible studies, group discussions and encounters in street ministry. It was thrilling to see the kind of maturity that was being produced in those new Christians, those added daily who were being saved.

I had been "church keeping" for years and had never seen that kind of wholesome growth before. I had members sitting in Sunday-school classes for forty years who still didn't have a clue as to what Christ had saved them from or saved them for! And here were these street Christians who had come to an amazing grasp of the Christian calling, frequently within a very few weeks.

On the late night flight home, David sat silently trying to process all of the new and stretching experience, the élan of the revival and the unquestionable power of God in which we had been immersed during those days. He finally broke the silence and said, "Bob, you've got to do that with us!" I asked for an explanation of what it was that I *had* to do. He explained that he really wanted to spend time with me in learning the Scriptures and the other factors that would set him free to be the Lord's disciple. And he felt that there were others in the congregation that also had that hungering.

That request was a catalyst in a process that had been going on in me for years. It was the request to become a disciple and a disciplemaker, to get out from behind the pulpit and to invest myself in others. But to do that I had to come to grips with what that involved, lest I create some grotesque caricatures of what God's new creation should look like.

If you will allow me to be your "long-distance" disciplemaker, maybe I can suggest some directions for your quest. But, first, let me suggest three prerequisites.

First, don't automatically screen out your pastor as a part of your discipling process. He or she may be a very hungry brother or sister who also longs for a discipling relationship and will have some gifts to bring to that process.

Second, the disciplemaking process is always done most effectively in a small group. There may be others who would accept an invitation in a minute to join you. These small groups or discipleship groups have been a tried and true instrument of Christian growth throughout church history.

And, third, make it a priority and give yourself a couple of years to work through the basics. It takes time to go from milk to strong meat. Strength and maturity don't happen overnight. As Eugene Peterson notes in *A Long Obedience in the Same Direction,* character and Christian fullness are the result of reorganizing your life in order to be free to seek first the kingdom of God and his justice.[1]

Douglas Southall Freeman, noted newspaper editor and Civil War historian, noted once that most of the significant things done in the world were done by persons who were either too busy or sick! There are few ideal and leisurely settings for the disciplines of growth.

But if the building of the church is the agenda of Jesus Christ, and if God the Father is able to do far more than we can comprehend according to his power at work in us to bring glory to himself in the church—then, lest we spend our lives on that which is naught, there is something we need to get straight right off the bat. We need to be singleminded about the task of becoming those instruments of his praise who are skillful, free, usable, joyful and holy.

Listen! I don't want this to sound ominous or heavy. I don't want to suggest that to be a disciple requires that you be a scholar. But it does require that you worship the Lord with all of your heart and mind and soul and strength.

And if you can't find anyone or any others to share the adventure with you right away, then become a do-it-yourselfer. Become "the Lord's troubadour" in your church community.

Four Areas of Discipline

Let me suggest four areas of discipline that will need to be a part of your discipleship. I learned them from the Order of St. Benedict, and then added one on my own. The Benedictines call them "formations," but I will call them simply disciplines. These four are interdependent and also nurture each other:

1. *The discipline of knowing the King (or spiritual formation).* This is the development of your relationship with Jesus, our Great King. Do you know him? Is your relationship with him alive, growing, healthy and transforming?

2. *The discipline of knowing our New Testament faith (or theological formation).* Do you know what God is like, what his character and will are? Do you understand the gospel of the kingdom of God and what it means to "believe into Christ"?

3. *The discipline of being called to be sent (or formation for Christian witness).* This is the discipline of knowing how we become agents of the gospel of the kingdom in the human community. What is your calling? What are you sent to do? How do you relate to the world around you?

4. *The disciplines of Christian community (or formation for Christian community).* These are the disciplines of living fruitfully within the community of Christ's people. How has that community, that church, expressed itself over the centuries? How do you relate to other pilgrim-adventurers in the always-in-process-and-never-perfect family of God?

These four need to be kept in balance if our discipleship, and hence our ministry within the family of God, is to be wholesome. We can be entirely competent in one and a complete klutz in another. I knew a couple of church folk once who had literally memorized tomes of theology and would spit it out on a moment's provocation on any subject—like putting a nickel into a theological juke box! But apart from that, they were essentially useless to the witness of the congregation.

The Discipline of Knowing the King

Jesus came proclaiming the gospel of God: "The time has come; the kingdom of God is upon you; repent, and believe the Gospel" (Mk 1:14-15 NEB).

A few decades later Peter told the scattered and exiled Christians, "In your hearts set apart Christ as Lord" (1 Pet 3:15 NIV).

Both of these calls speak of the same reality. Mark's account is thrilling. Jesus comes announcing that the long-awaited reign of God, the messianic dominion, the age to come, has come into this present age, this present dominion of darkness—and that it has come in his own person. And when the Great King arrives, the only acceptable response is to turn from all other loyalties and give oneself in devotion and trust and loyalty to that king. So Jesus says, Repent and believe in the joyous news.

This discipline of knowing the King, then, has to do with your wholehearted and knowledgeable relationship with God the Father through Jesus Christ, the Son, and your openness to the transforming work of the Holy Spirit within you. It has to do with willingly and joyously owning Jesus as Lord, with lovingly yielding to his sovereign lordship. It is to quit arguing with him and then to invite him to indwell you and to recreate you into his own image and for his own purpose. This is the call to holiness.

Holiness is that relationship of integrity with the character and will of God. It involves a reorientation of our whole lives—a continual conversion if you will. It is not always without pain. But it is always beautiful and it is always in process.

Repentance is dynamic. We keep discovering ideologies and alien loyalties that are part of the darkness. They may be intellectual idols, or political and economic principalities. Sometimes enculturation, darkness and death inhabit the church.

And faith is also dynamic. It continues to lay hold of the wonder of God himself, and that wonder and knowledge is marvelously liberating.

Yet, to come to receive Jesus Christ, and to be received by him, it is essential that we know, first of all, the central *data* concerning his life and ministry and his call to us. Jesus warned against making easy or trifling decisions. He told us to count the cost.

To put it baldly, there is something very radical and altogether other about faith in Jesus. It runs counter to all of the loyalties and agendas of this age. So it is critical for us to know exactly who this person is, and this is a fathomless process of discovery.

We also need to understand that Christ makes *demands* on us to which we must submit. As we noted above, Jesus always prefaces his call to faith with the call to repentance. He commands us to repent, to change the direction of our thinking and living so that we are in harmony with him (Acts 17:30).

Only then are we privileged to enter into the *promises* of the joyous news of the kingdom. Grace is rich and free, but it is not cheap and unprincipled! "Not everyone who says to me, 'Lord, Lord,' will enter the kingdom of heaven, but only he who does the will of my Father who is in heaven" (Mt 7:21 NIV). Grace, forgiveness, new life, peace and joy are promises of the kingdom, and they are offered by the king to those who acknowledge his sovereign reign in their lives and in the world.

Then, too, we must acknowledge that the call to faith in Jesus Christ as Lord is not a call to a solitary faith, but a call into a *community* of faith. Note in the Pentecost sermon and in the response the call to baptism, to go public with the faith, and through baptism to become part of a new community, the church (Acts 2:38-47).

Data, demands, promises and community are essential parts of knowing him. But never forget that the point of all of this is *knowing him!*

It is all too easy and common to reduce knowing Christ to knowing a set of doctrinal propositions or conforming to the ideological expression of a particular Christian enclave. Jesus said, "Come unto me," and we must nurture this relationship with him, with the God of our salvation who has come to us in Jesus Christ.

Who is this One to whom I come? What is he like? What is his heart? What is his character? How has he made himself known and how has he made himself vulnerable? How does he love? And what grieves him? What does he say about me—and us? How does he view the world in which we live?

The place to begin in our disciplines for getting to know the King is the Scriptures, and especially the teachings of Jesus and the apostles who were with him.

But we can also profit through the community of faith as it has expressed its relationship with the Lord God over all of these centuries. The writings of other Christians help me to keep my filters clean and are one of the blessings of the communion of the saints. So here are a few writings that have helped me. I choose mostly contemporary works so that they will be in print, but they will suggest to you other works that may be found by searching.

A basic study of our biblical faith is John Stott's *Basic Christianity*, which is written to serious inquirers, but is a good refresher, and I walk through it periodically for my own benefit.[2] Significant in my life also is the classical work *The Cost of Discipleship* by the German martyr, Dietrich Bonhoeffer.[3] This one is worth the effort and will take you below the surface.

For a very broad spectrum of Christian devotion, and a reading discipline on a weekly basis Reuben Job and Norman Shawchuck have put together *A Guide to Prayer for Ministers and Other Servants*,[4] which is a collection of hymns, writings and scriptural readings following the church year and encompassing the whole diverse spectrum of the Christian church over several centuries.

I think that any contemporary adventurer needs to read the Christian faith through the eyes of the third, or two-thirds, world, where Christian faith walks perilous paths. I have found the Catholic priest-theologian Segundo Galilea fascinating in giving me new eyes for Jesus in his works *Following Jesus* and *The Beatitudes: To Evangelize As Jesus Did.*[5]

John White has written a helpful study on the Christian life called simply *The Fight,* which puts a lot of the pieces in place. And, frankly, I find Calvin Miller's poetic metaphor in *The Singer, The Song* and *The Finale* to be enormously provocative in my appreciation of the love and ministry of Jesus.[6]

These writers will in turn bring you to other writers. They can nurture you in barren times. I learned this discipline of reading from my father, a busy engineer, who with deliberateness worked his way through volumes of Christian classics by reading a few pages, putting in a bookmark, getting back to it a week later, and over the years becoming one of the most literate Christians I know. Give yourself three to six months, for instance, on these, then move on.

The Discipline of Knowing Our New Testament Faith

One of our modern poets spoke of so many in our society "who have not one thought to rub against another while waiting for the train." John Stott regularly urges his listeners to avoid at all costs, what he describes as a "mind-less Christianity." We are not likely to be of much help in renewing congregations in life and power if we are part of the mindlessness of so much of contemporary evangelicalism.

Our primary quest must be to have a living grasp of the message of the Holy Scriptures. They are our primary data, our authoritative guide and God's unique instrument for making himself known to us. Jesus and the apostles held the Scriptures in high esteem, and so must we.

But as for you, continue in what you have learned and have become convinced of, because you know those from whom you learned it, and how from infancy you have known the holy Scriptures, which are able to make you wise for salvation through faith in Christ Jesus. All Scripture is God-breathed and is useful for teaching, rebuking, correcting and training in right-eousness, so that the man of God may be thoroughly equipped for every good work. (2 Tim 3:14-16 NIV)

What every disciple needs, then, is a regular, disciplined, prayer-ful, thoughtful time of fellowship with God through the study of Scripture. If you need assistance in this, perhaps you will profit by the tried and true ministry of Scripture Union, which produces brief aids to disciplined Bible study that take you through Scrip-ture over a several year period.[7]

You will probably need also a good introduction to Scripture so that you don't get lost in the cultural and textual mysteries of this awesome set of writings. Our whole encounter with Scripture be-comes more fulfilling if we have some understanding of the con-text, cultures, purpose and literary nuances of the writings, though any sincere believer can pick up Scripture and be rewarded by reading its pages.

Along with the disciplined study of Scripture itself, then, I would suggest *Knowing Scripture* by R. C. Sproul and, if that doesn't satisfy your appetite, *How to Study the Bible for All Its Worth* by Gordon D. Fee and Douglas Stuart (this is a bit more academic, but superb in content).[8]

From another angle, it helps to know something of the story line of Scripture. What's the message? Why is God doing and saying all these things over all these centuries? Any one of the following four books, from three different Christian traditions, will serve to give you the clues you are looking for: *The Kingdom of God* by John Bright is the classic (Reformed tradition); my own *Joy to the World* follows in that tradition; *The Upside-Down Kingdom*, by Donald B. Kraybill (Anabaptist tradition) is very provocative and readable; and Bishop Mortimer Arias's *Announcing the Reign of God* (Methodist tradition) is in the same vein as Kraybill but reflects a Latin American perspective.[9] All of these, I might note, see that the message of the reign/kingdom of God is the key to understanding the Old and New Testaments.

Along with the content and message of Scripture, you, as an adventurer and a renewer in the church, will want to know something of the church's history and beliefs. This needs to be more than a provincial study of your own corner of the church and its history. Instead you will want a broad sweep of who we are as God's people, what we as the whole church believe, and where we come from.

For a history of the church you cannot do better than to read Martin Marty's *A Short History of Christianity.*[10] You will find all kinds of fascinating main highways and sidestreets in this volume. The Christian family has moments of ecstasy and times of horrifying scandal, and they help us today to see ourselves in the fabric of God's purpose (as we noted in chapter two). Add to this, if you will, *Knowing God* by J. I. Packer as a statement of the church's understanding of God.[11] This will break you out of truncated and trivializing understandings of God, and walk you into a new depth of devotion.

A few months in this discipline and then on to the next. But let me say that a Christian can be ever so articulate in Scripture and in Christian doctrine, and yet not be a worshiper, a channel for God's rivers of life-giving waters or a wholesome witness to God's saving purpose for the world. The knowledge of the riches of God's grace should lead us to new devotion and to new obedience. The purpose of this knowledge is that God's Spirit will use it to remake us in the likeness of God's Son, into paradigms of the kingdom of God.

The Discipline of Being Called to Be Sent

Whenever the church forgets that it has been called by Jesus Christ to be sent forth again into the world as salt and light, it atrophies. Jesus said, "As the Father has sent me, I am sending you" (Jn 20:21 NIV). We have, unfortunately, interpreted that text to mean professional, crosscultural, missionary calling and sending. But all of us are called with a holy calling so that God can thrust us again into the brokenness of this present age as agents of the age to come.

As adventurers in Christian obedience, we need to get equipped and comfortable in this calling. This is the natural witness which we have as God's new creation.

This responsibility goes beyond verbal witnessing. We are sent to live out God's design in a new community called the church. The bulk of the New Testament, let it be noticed, does not deal with the overt evangelistic task of the church, but rather with the creation of the community of faith, hope and love and the relationships within it. The church is to be a sign of God's kingdom and visible for all to see.

We are called also to be sent into the world as instruments of justice in God's hand. Our light is to shine so that men and women may see our good works and comprehend that God is doing a new thing and working out a wonderful new design in the midst of humankind.

This sending by our Lord is where the real challenge of the adventure of discipleship begins. It is for this that we are called.

For starts, and for delightful reading, try Becky Pippert's *Out of the Saltshaker*.[12] This introduces you to the ministry of sharing our wonder at and love for Jesus with others. Beyond that, walk through *Thank God It's Monday* by William Diehl and *Called to Holy Worldliness* by Richard Mouw—both in a series on the ministry of the laity, which will get your mouth watering to be Christ's persons in the Monday morning world.[13]

And because it is so easy to get into bad habits in our thinking about the outreach of the Christian church, I have been prodded and challenged and provoked by *Evangelizing Neopagan North America* by Al Krass.[14] Krass is a prophetic voice who though he needs to be read with discernment, certainly needs to be read!

But don't stop without reading *In the Gap: What It Means to Be a World Christian* by David Bryant.[15] There is a world out there beyond our congregation and beyond this neighborhood that the

Lord wants to reach. That'll get you started—and take a few months.

The Disciplines of Christian Community

What will it take to give us a vision of how we can be positive, serving, ministering, constructive, patient, strengthening members of the Christian community?

The classic work on Christian community in this century must be *Life Together* by Dietrich Bonhoeffer.[16] Most likely, because this work was written under the adverse circumstances of Nazi Germany, it reflects an awesome depth of understanding of what Christian community is all about. I have, in times past, literally read through this aloud in our small group, just because it is that important.

In a theological, yet practical vein, Howard Snyder's *Community of the King* is "must" reading.[17] At a less theoretical, more practical level, you need to read *Caring Enough to Confront* by David Augsburger (you'll learn why this is practical once you begin to be available for the renewal and transformation of congregations!) and *Getting Together: A Guide for Good Groups* by Em Griffin (this also will prove most helpful once you begin to generate small groups in your church).[18]

And for a postgraduate course for the brave and bold, any adventurer in the revitalization of the Christian church ought to read Richard Lovelace's classic on the theology of renewal, *Dynamics of Spiritual Life,* a marvelous combination of church history, Scripture, theology, and insights into church renewal. His more recent *Renewal as a Way of Life* might be a good point of entry into his thinking. It provides discussion questions together with parallel reading in *Dynamics.*[19]

I know of some, and have heard of other, groups of men and women who meet together on a periodic basis with a contract between them to read a book, such as some of these mentioned, and discuss it. Some of them meet for early breakfast, some over lunch, some in home meetings—but they are equipping themselves to bring new joy into their congregations. The disciplines of Christian community require, by the very nature of the subject, that you, if at all possible, engage another or a few others to join you in prayer, discussion, study, in mutual refining and in doing what you are sent by Christ to do. This can also have delightful social dimensions. Such ad hoc disciplemaking groups can become the focus of remarkable friendships.

A disciple who cannot relate to others in community will never be a part of transforming the family of God!

These four areas of discipline and disciplemaking are the place to start. If you can deliberately and patiently stake out this territory, take the first steps, and give yourself a couple of years, you will have the tools to begin the Pioneer Plunge into the intoxicating adventure of being one of the conductors of God's renewing grace and power into your congregation. Sometimes it's lonely, sometimes it requires patient plodding, but you cannot imagine the fulfillment that will result from your prayers and work.

5
Toward a Kingdom-shaped Community

Marilou was sitting in my den under some duress. Her talking to me was an agreement she had made in exchange for being given lodging in the home of a Christian couple. Her life had been a disaster from the very beginning. She had never known any domestic stability or security. She was an unwanted child—one of many in her family. She had taken up with a man and lived with him in a bizarre set of circumstances replete with drugs.

The problem was that she had no capacity to even visualize what love, permanence, family or domestic beauty looked like! The fact that a man let her sleep with him was the closest thing to love and security she could imagine. My attempts to call her into some semblance of the newness and freedom of Christian life and Christian understandings of love and family were like talking into a void. It was an exercise in frustration. I never did get through to her. She longed for domestic stability, but she couldn't imagine it and later ran away again, and we have lost contact with her.

I have found the same dilemma in teaching the membership enrichment class for our congregation. Candidates for membership come from many places and with a great diversity of church backgrounds. The church has been a part of the social fabric of their lives and therefore is important to them, but few can make any connection between that meaningful experience and Jesus Christ and his kingdom. They have had little more than a mundane institutional experience within the church, so they are not excited about the role of the church in the world.

Ironically, even some of the apostles of church renewal are questing for a reality that they have never experienced. I have frequently asked these friends to define for me exactly what they thought a renewed or vital church would look like, only to receive unfocused answers that indicated a hungering and a reaching out, more than any precise awareness or experience of the renewal they sought.

Lest we be in the same quandary as Marilou or my membership candidates, we need to be quite deliberate in seeking some legitimate and biblical vision of what a kingdom-of-God-shaped community should look like.

We need to be like skillful art restorers who now with some high-tech equipment can see beneath layers of paint to a masterpiece on a piece of canvas. Over many years, this person and that have added to, or changed, or sought to redo the masterpiece until it lies obscured under untold layers of additions.

The restorer has to go to work with skill and gentleness to slowly remove all of those layers, careful not to harm the original. This can be tedious, but the presence of the masterpiece motivates him or her to spend the months and years to arrive at the master's painting.

The same kind of obscuring process happens again and again to the church as the community of God's new creation in Christ. Persons—some with good and sincere intent, and some with malice and dark motivation—add to and take away from God's intended design until the church scarcely resembles the dwelling place of God by the Holy Spirit. It becomes focused on its buildings. Or a clergy caste develops, which redefines the role of the people of God. Worship devolves into religious entertainment, and traditional religion begins to replace the dynamic of living faith in the God and Father of our Lord Jesus Christ. Signs and wonders give way to organizational skill. The congregation sings about being lost in wonder, love and praise, but can scarcely imagine it.

A. W. Tozer, a generation ago, explained the church's malaise. He explained that Jesus, this executed criminal, after his resurrection, gave his followers an impossible command to go make disciples of all nations. Incredibly they took him seriously, and the church empowered by the Holy Spirit moved out in power to accomplish this task. In a delightful turn of phrase Tozer noted that as long as they moved in obedience, they moved also in power, but when they stopped moving and dug in to preserve their gain, "like the manna in the wilderness they bred worms and stank!"

However it happens, it does happen again and again. The darkness intrudes the community of light and obscures its beauty. Merely human agendas gain ascendancy, and the joy and power of the gospel become mere tradition, if not relics.

In C. S. Lewis's *Prince Caspian*, the Pevensie children, who had been kings and queens in the land of Narnia in its golden era, are magically summoned back. In England where they lived, only a few months had passed, but in the "other world" of Narnia centuries had passed. Such was the mystery and magic of Narnia. But as they arrive back in Narnia everything looks strange and wild. They find themselves in an ancient ruin and on a raised pavement. As they are surviving their first night in the ruin and making do with roasted apples, more scorched than roasted, they begin to wonder why some of the setting seems so familiar. Then the light dawns on Peter and he explains to them that this ruin was their ancient castle of Cair Paravel. Sure enough, beneath the ivy-encrusted wall behind them they find a door, and breaking through the rotting door they find the stairs down into the ancient treasure chamber, where their armor and jewels and weapons and finery are stored.

So it is with the church. Hidden in the ruins of the most disastrous appearing church are the treasures of the gospel. Behind doors of tradition whose meaning is long forgotten are the riches of God's good purpose in Christ. In hymns unsung, or sung without mind or heart, are the devotional jewels of saints now made perfect. In creeds relegated to dusty shelves lie the great struggles in the church's faith, often written in agony and sealed with blood.

Our purpose here, then, is to clear our vision, to look with anointed eyes at the Scriptures and the wholesome traditions of the church, and to see, if we can, what God intends for his people so that our efforts at restoring and refreshing will be owned and blessed by him.

Adventurers in the church need to be able to see visions and dream dreams—to look for the city with foundations whose architect and builder is God. We need to arrive at some sense of the revolutionary nature of the church in God's design, a vision that will make our mouths water and motivate us, like the pearl of great price in Jesus' teachings, to press on through conflict and discouragement to realize that vision.

We desperately need this vision because ecclesiastical systems and structures don't usually change quickly. When you seek to turn the church in a more kingdom-oriented direction, as in turning a great ocean liner, you have to keep the pressure on the rudder.

So where do we begin?

Biblical Images and Metaphors

The Bible contains some striking images of the church. The fact that the church is, and has always been, very human and imperfect should not dissuade us from pursuing biblical norms. We need continually to search the Scriptures to see what God wants us to be and to do. If, as we explore these biblical images, you find little evidence of these characteristics in your particular congregation, then recognize it may take a long time before you see them come to life. If they are present, though qualified and stunted, then they may emerge more quickly into full bloom.

The images or descriptions that we shall explore here are like several facets of a single diamond. Often through the very same Scripture passage you will discern several different images of what the church is all about (see, for example, 1 Pet 2:4-10).

As our vision is clarified and we are able to discern both the mystery of the church and what God has ordained it to demonstrate to the world, we will be able to work our way out of cultural overlays and unbiblical accretions. Then we will begin to approximate God's true intent for his people, his chosen people and his holy nation.

The Family of God

Right away in the beginning of his gospel account, John says: "But to all who did receive him, to those who have yielded him their allegiance, he gave the right to become children of God, not born of any human stock, or by the fleshly desire of a human father, but the offspring of God himself" (Jn 1:12-13 NEB). Implicit in the whole of the New Testament is the notion that we, through Jesus Christ, become God's family. In the extravagance of his love we are invited into his family through allegiance to his son. We are adopted into his own household and become heirs of God and joint heirs with Christ.

The designation "the family of God," as such, is not used in this passage, but the concept is clearly implied in the use of the phrase "children of God." Jesus teaches us to call God "our Father." By the Holy Spirit we address him as Father, or even more intimately as Abba, which is the Aramaic for "Daddy." I've never gotten used to addressing God my Father as "Daddy," but there it is.

This family language is not confined to our relationship to God as Father. The apostles also use it as they speak to the Christian congregation as "children" (1 Cor 14:14; 1 Jn 2:1) and of themselves as "fathers" (1 Cor 4:15). This, of course, gives validity to the use of the title "father" to leaders within the Christian community. But by far the most common designation to those who are with us in the family of God is that they are sisters and brothers.

Do you remember the account of the timid but faithful Ananias (Acts 9:10-19)? The Lord spoke to him in a vision and told him to go and lay hands on the blinded Saul of Tarsus and speak God's word to him. Imagine Ananias's trepidations at that commission. Nevertheless he went and found Saul and then, in one of the heart-touching episodes in Scripture, spoke the word of affirmation and family acceptance to him, "Brother Saul, the Lord—Jesus, who appeared to you on the road as you were coming here—has sent me so that you may see again and be filled with the Holy Spirit" (Acts 9:17 NIV). To this devastated person, now humbled and converted, the word of familial acceptance and love: *Brother Saul!*

In other places the Scriptures call for brotherly and sisterly affection (Rom 12:10; 2 Pet 1:7). What does all of this mean for the church?

It means, first of all, that our new life is from God. We are born of God. In this new family we have heavenly parentage. We are children by his gracious initiative. As a result we are *bound together* under his authority by willing submission and affection. We are not like a group of orphans, uncertain of parentage or of family authority, left to squabble among ourselves.

No, because we know who we are and who our Father is, we are also secure enough in his love and grace to work through all of our sibling tensions.

It is this family assumption that underlies all of the relational instructions of the New Testament. Just look at those occasions in the early church when there was a matter of difference or conflict. What does the church do? It stops, gathers together, goes to the Father in prayer, submits to his authority and resolves the matter in brotherly affection.

I have been learning this lesson slowly over my lifetime. I tend to be strong-minded on something I feel is right. But so do others.

One of the most helpful things when tempers got short and two opinions dug in for the showdown has been for one of my leadership team to say gently, "Bob, why don't we stop and pray before we go any further? God doesn't want us hurting each other, and we need to find out what his purpose for us is!" Sure enough, when we have just rested it there and refused to make any decision until we all feel good about it in the Father's presence, good things have happened.

As the family of God, the church is also a community of people who understand themselves and their reason for being in reference to the character and will of their Father. The Father's character and will determine who and what his family, the church, should be. "Our Father in heaven, holy is your name. Your kingdom come. Your will be done."

You see this principle very clearly in Ephesians 5:1-2: "Therefore be imitators of God, as beloved children. And walk in love, as Christ loved us and gave himself up for us, a fragrant offering and sacrifice to God" (RSV). Look at Jesus, the firstborn among many brethren, who as the obedient son, yielded himself up to do the will of his Father: "Lo, I have come to do thy will" (Heb 10:7 RSV). The Scriptures make plain that it is in the doing of the will of our heavenly Father that we enter the kingdom of God (Mt 7:21) and that we are to be perfect as our heavely Father is perfect (Mt 5:48). This is all to say that the Father expects his family likeness to be reproduced in those who are his offspring by the Holy Spirit.

Because of this family relationship, your congregation or the smaller renewal group within your congregation is to be a unit of God's family. There his love, his authority, his character, his grace, his agenda are to be your common bond. We belong to each other in the family of God. We are brothers and sisters to each other in all which that means in affection, in rebuke and reproof, in caring, in responsibility, in shared lives, and in mutual zeal for the honor of our Father's name. There must be no individualism, privatism and autonomy in the new community in Jesus Christ. In this household of faith we are obligated to each other to lead lives of self-denial and mutual affection.

The Body of Christ

The "body of Christ" is one of the most familiar New Testament images of the church (see Rom 12; 1 Cor 12; Eph 1, 3—5; and Col 1—3). The uses in Romans and Corinthians tend to focus on the diversity and interdependence of the members, while those in Ephesians and Colossians focus on Christ, who is the head of the body. Through the body metaphor we see that the gifts and ministries given by the Holy Spirit to individuals are for the blessing of the whole community, designed to bring the whole body to maturity in Christ, the head.

There is obviously a great deal of mystery in the body of Christ and in the use of the figure. Yet, over the centuries through wide-ranging discussions and interpretations of this image, several things are obvious:

    a. Christ is present in the world through a visible, physical community, which he indwells and animates by his Holy Spirit.

    b. This organism is a spiritual one in which the individual members share a common life through diverse functions and are growing toward maturity, which is the "measure of the stature of the fullness of Christ."

    c. It is only as each unique part functions properly that the whole body grows and matures into Christ, who is the head.

In recent years the use of the term *body life* has brought this image into the forefront in many congregations, and this is to be applauded.[1] It has enabled the Christian community to move away from the erroneous concept of a passive laity with an active and magisterial clergy, which has plagued the church. It raises to high visibility the unique ministry which every one of the members of the body has. It makes each person's healthy faith and function a matter of importance to the rest of the body.

At this point we need to remind ourselves that the body is both local and universal—but it is not sectarian! The body of Christ is not Baptist, Catholic or Episcopalian, however rich these traditions are within the body. We all belong to each other and to our mutual head, who is Christ.

A Dwelling Place of God in the Spirit

If the family image teaches us the relational qualities of our life together and the body image speaks to the interdependence between members as they exercise gifts, then the description of the church as the *dwelling place of God in the Spirit* (Eph 2:22) lifts up the dynamic character of the people of God.

What makes the church qualitatively different from merely human communities is not only its creation by Christ but also its dynamic, supernatural indwelling by the Holy Spirit. This is exciting beyond words. Paul almost takes your breath away when he says, "This power working in us is the same as the mighty strength which he used when he raised Christ from death and seated him at his right side in the heavenly world" (Eph 1:19-20 TEV).

God dwells in his church by the Holy Spirit. The church is called the temple of the Holy Spirit (1 Cor 3:16-17). It is empowered by the Spirit, and to be involved with the church is somehow to taste of the powers of the age to come by being partakers of the Holy Spirit (Heb 6:4-5). The Holy Spirit enables the church to pray, and at the same time he intercedes for the church. The Holy Spirit is Christ's gift to the church, and through this same Spirit gifts are given to each member of the church for the mutual encouragement and upbuilding of the whole. The Spirit reproduces in us the characteristics of the Father and the Son, and these are called the fruit of the Holy Spirit (Gal 5:22-23). He is the source of the church's unity: we are one in the Spirit!

All in all, this description of the church as being alive in and by the Holy Spirit opens our vision to a dimension of congregational life and impact that fairly thrills and throbs with power and awe.

How can the Christian community ever be tame or dull when it is indwelt, animated, empowered, unified, purified and given access to the mind of God by the Holy Spirit? Even in all of the church's imperfections, its "in process" immaturity, it is unique. Therefore in our adventure, our Pioneer Plunge in far-from-perfect congregations, we join in the excitement of the church through the ages as we pray: Veni Creator Spiritus! Come Creator Spirit!

A Servant People

Nothing messes up the health of the church more than petty and power-hungry folk. The antidote for such a problem comes in this next definition or image—that of a *servant* people. Implicit in all of the descriptions we have examined thus far is the fact that the people of God are to be conformed to the likeness of Jesus Christ. The Holy Spirit indwells us so that we may be empowered to live Christ. We must not miss the thrust of this. It is far too congenial to our perverse natures to conjure up all kinds of images of the likeness of Christ in terms of spirituality, prestige, religious superiority and ecclesiastical one-upmanship. We often have very fuzzy ideas of what it means to believe into Christ.

So, hear his own words: "A dispute also arose among them, which of them was to be regarded as the greatest. And he said to them, 'The kings of the Gentiles exercise lordship over them; and those in authority over them are called benefactors. But not so with you; rather let the greatest among you become as the youngest, and the leader as one who serves. For which is greater, one who sits at table, or one who serves? Is it not the one who sits at table? But I am among you as one who serves' " (Lk 22:24-27 RSV).

How easily the church forgets! Jesus' whole teaching on the way to achieve, to be fruitful, to get ahead in the kingdom of God is an upside-down principle. It is that we should deny ourselves and become servants, even as he did (Jn 12:23-26). One factor that may render so many congregations sterile is that they have been indifferent to this call to servanthood.

We are to be the servant people of the servant Lord. When the congregation at Philippi was getting all snarled up in some internecine disputes, what did Paul write? "Have this mind among yourselves, which is yours in Christ Jesus, who, though he was in the form of God, did not account equality with God a thing to be grasped, but emptied himself, taking the form of a servant, being born in the likeness of men" (Phil 2:5-7 RSV).

There are, and always have been, some who covet special empowerings of the Holy Spirit and the exercise of spiritual gifts so that they may achieve some stature as "Spirit-filled" persons. But the empowering of the Holy Spirit is not for self-gratification. It is for servanthood. The anointing of the Holy Spirit is for costly obedience and service in the likeness of Jesus. We are given grace to be a servant people. That theme rings loud and clear in Scripture.

The Community of the Kingdom of God

The great description of the gospel in the New Testament (especially in Matthew, Mark and Luke) is that it is the thrilling news of the kingdom of God. All through the pages of the New Testament this theme throbs, sometimes dramatically and sometimes in subtle paraphrase. But recognizing that the Lord God has come to establish his messianic reign in the person of Jesus Christ and that we are to seek first the kingdom of God and his righteousness opens up all kinds of fascinating and revolutionary implications for our Christian adventure.

Yet we are bound to ask how this theme relates to the church. Is the church synonymous with the kingdom of God? Are all of the hymns we sing about the kingdom of God, in reality, hymns about the church? Not really! The kingdom of God is far more all-encompassing than the church. And yet they are related.

The church is, in fact, the community of the kingdom of God. Or, as Herman Ridderbos has stated it: "Thus the [church] is the community of those who, as the true people of God, receive the gifts of the kingdom of heaven provisionally now already since the Messiah has come, and one day in the state of perfection at the parousia [appearing] of the Son of Man."[2]

So the church is the community of the kingdom of God, and this adds a great deal of exciting color to our study of the church. The reality of the "age to come" which is upon us, or the kingdom of God drawn nigh in the advent of Jesus the Messiah, means that the church as the community of the kingdom of God is a community of people who have willingly submitted themselves to the reign of God. Here is a people who have an understanding of the historic and cosmic significance of the coming of Christ. Here are those who recognize his divine sovereignty, who have in repentance forsaken every alien authority and who joyfully serve him as their redeemer and as their Lord.

In this community, which we call the church, then, the gospel of the kingdom of God is on display. The community becomes a *sign* of the kingdom of God, or an *evidence* of the kingdom of God. It is a clue to the watching world of what the kingdom is all about. The New Testament writers joyfully affirm that the word of the kingdom is not just talk, but power. And from this self-awareness comes the wholesome moral, intellectual, ethical and eschatological flavor of the community of the kingdom, which is the church.

This means that we are not so much a people experiencing salvation (though we are that in the fullest sense) as we are a people under authority to our king, who is also our savior from the alien kingdom of darkness. A new order has come in Jesus Christ. The king has come! And by repentance and faith we have entered into that kingdom and so rejoice to be citizens together in the community of the Great King.

It is natural to ask exactly how the church is a sign of the kingdom. In recent years the church has identified several visible expressions of its life which say to the watching world that we are people of an alternative dominion. These expressions should be cultivated in your congregational life.

1. The church's focus on the living God in worship and adoration *(leitourgia),* speaks to the world of the source and object of our kingdom faith.

2. The unselfish, caring, costly and interdependent relation-

ship of believers to one another *(koinonia)* is also evidence that we are disciples of the Lord of love, Jesus Christ.

3. The church's preaching *(kerygma)*, its heralding of the message of Jesus Christ, informs all that the church believes and does, and explains the meaning of the kingdom of God to the world.

4. The church's compassionate ministry to human need *(diakonia)*, its ministry of good news to the poor, its ministry of justice and peacemaking, its care for the hungry, naked, imprisoned and sick are evidences of kingdom priorities.

5. Finally, as the people of the kingdom of God engage in kingdom behavior, there is that joyous and contagious spoken witness *(martyria)* which explains our lives, which evangelizes, and which draws women and men to the joy of the kingdom of God, to faith and forgiveness and to the new creation.

The church needs to realize that this kingdom faith makes us a troublesome lot. Since we are always and primarily citizens of the kingdom of God, our first loyalty is elsewhere than in the kingdoms, nationalities, principalities and powers of this present age. The subtitle of Bishop Mortimer Arias's book on the reign of God is "Evangelization and the Subversive Memory of Jesus" which pinpoints the nature of our Christian witness, of kingdom evangelicalism—namely, that it is in the most wholesome and redemptive sense subversive.

And because of that, in some way we are always strangers in the l of our sojourn. Jesus is Lord! The kingdoms of this world are always seen for what they are. We are therefore a prophetic people. We are, on one hand, salt and light and redemptive citizens in our society. On the other hand we are not passively uncritical of these present governments and their policies. Yet we are most positively those who bring light and joy and meaning to this present age under death. We are the expression of the creative and recreative character of the kingdom of God right here in this man scene, right here in Babylon, right here in River City. Our neighbors have a right to look at us and see fleshed out in us that behavior, those relationships, that understanding of human events, that faith and hope and love that is characteristic of the kingdom of God.

So we have walked through a potpourri of biblical images of the church in an attempt to know at least what we are looking for, to know what a kingdom-shaped community should look like. This is what the church in its integrity and vigor should approximate. We know that it will always be in process and never perfect. But these images will shape our life and witness in the church and point the direction to church renewal.

Having said that, we need to remind ourselves of two things again before we move on:

1. A real conversion is needed if we are to live together in the kind of community we have been describing from Scripture. Self-sufficiency is a secular ideal which influences Christians far too much. We try to be islands, a body within ourselves, all of which is a distortion. We fear dependency, loss of privacy or loss of personality. We fear that our patterns of selfishness will be revealed. It is no wonder that Jesus told his disciples that a grain of wheat, if it is to bear fruit, must first fall into the ground and die.

2. There is a continual proclivity on the part of the community of light to retrogress back to the darkness, of the community of the aeon of life to be enculturated and so conformed to the aeon of death. Because of this danger, the church must regularly re-examine its birthright, must regularly look afresh at Scripture, as we have done, and catch a fresh vision of the wonder of our calling to be a holy nation, a people who exist joyfully and heartily in conformity to the character and will of the gracious Lord who calls us.

Now on to the revolution!

6

Redemptive Subversion: Prayer & Faith

About this point you may be asking, "Why all this heady, cerebral stuff? When will we get down to business?"

Soon enough, but the historical and biblical backgrounds on the nature of the church that we have looked at are important. Without that kind of base, we are apt to launch into our project like the local Cub Scout pack, setting about to paint the house of the widowed and indigent Mrs. Anselm. They meant well, but they didn't understand scraping, sanding, priming or drop cloths. The result was not only paint in the wrong places—paint on the porch roof, paint on the walks—but broken shrubbery and other efforts that would soon need repeating because of untreated surfaces. Good will is not always sufficient. So it is important to know the territory and to gain some basic knowledge and skills.

But there is another lesson to learn as well. Churches have a life of their own. They have established and entrenched traditions, some obvious and some hidden. They have structures of leadership and often formal ties to denominational authorities. They have tenured members and organizations, and networks of decision making and influence.

They are all too much like the Confederate Army at Fredericksburg, a unit of Tennessee sharpshooters lying entrenched behind a stone wall on an elevation. Frontal assaults seldom succeed in situations like this, as General Burnside and the Union Army sorrily discovered.

So, rather than operating like assault troops, we need to operate like redemptive subversives. Subversives operate out of sight, yet with a very definite objective. They don't march in waving banners and heralding their intentions. Our design then is to begin the process of transforming our own far-from-ideal congregation into something that looks and feels and smells like the community of the kingdom of God. To do this we offer ourselves to be the agents of God's gracious life, truth and power within whatever congregation we find ourselves.

How do we do this in a way that doesn't draw attention to itself and yet is effective? In effect, we are asking, How do we outflank the congregation's dead structures? Or, to look at the problem another way, we are dealing with congregations that lack essential ingredients in their corporate lives. When these ingredients are introduced, they begin to transform the whole.

I see this in my own yard. We have very poor soil—an acidic pipe clay. I know that for healthy plants to grow, then, I need to introduce compost to create tilth. I need to do a lab test to see what it lacks in such elements as nitrogen, phosphorus and potash. Then I need to create a reasonable acid-alkaline balance. This doesn't happen overnight. As a matter of fact it takes years to create a good bed. There are no shortcuts around the time and labor that it takes to introduce into this soil those elements that make it fertile, friable and fruitful.

The same is true of different congregations. Some have more healthy ingredients than others. Some appear to have almost no good soil. But Scripture does not leave us in ignorance of what can transform congregational soil. And as God's redemptive subversives, we can begin to introduce the healthy ingredients into congregational life that God will use to transform it.

I don't think it really matters how barren your church appears, you can become the basic source of the nutrients that begin the change. And if there are two or three others who are available for this ministry, then praise God!

There are three elements critical to healthy congregational soil, soil that will produce kingdom-shaped community: *faith, love* and *hope*. Paul uses this trio almost like a formula (1 Cor 13:13; Eph 1:15-18; Col 1:3-5; 1 Thess 1:2-3; 2 Thess 1:3-4; and just *faith* and *love* in 1 Tim 1:15). Peter too puts them together (1 Pet 1:20-22).[1] They are absolutely basic to any healthy congregation. They are priority elements.

It is no happenstance that New Testament writers make so much over them. And what is more exciting is that they are places where you can begin, handles on which you can take hold, ministries in which you can be engaged, nutrients which you can produce, that will create healthy congregational soil out of which the gospel can express itself in community. But they cannot be developed apart from a commitment to prayer. So we shall take up prayer and faith in the remainder of this chapter and turn to love and hope in the next.

When You Don't Know What to Do

At a time when, to put it charitably, leanness of soul marked the congregation of which I was a part, a couple of friends suggested that the very least we could do was to meet regularly for prayer. We had no human handles on any of the discouraging attitudes and structures within the church. And the only time we could find in our busy schedules was at 6:30 in the morning. Practicality demanded we meet for breakfast in an all-night restaurant. The manager saved us a corner booth out of kindness, and we would arrive, give the waitress our order and then begin discussing the areas that needed our prayers and God's gracious intervention.

Our prayers were brief and to the point. Sometimes, I'm sure, the waitress didn't know what to make of this group, one looking out the window, one looking at the saltshaker, and one with his head bowed—anyone of which might be praying. But that simple praying went on for years, and I am fully persuaded that it was one of the key factors in the eventual transformation of that congregational wilderness into a very fruitful garden. And though I have long since moved away, I receive reports that the prayer is still going on, and so is the blessing.

Prayer is practical. Prayer creates a climate within a congregation, a climate of readiness. We really should not say anything about congregational transformation, or congregational fruitfulness, if we think we can achieve it by techniques or tinkering. If you as a person or as a group have not prayed for God's blessing on your congregation, then your primary duty has been left undone.

We need to go before him, to whom all things are naked and open, and ask what has caused the desolation we see and what we can do to begin to turn things around. Prayer is one of the most practical ministries that God has given to his people.

If the congregation in which you are trying to survive is fruitless and infested with alien presences, content with meaningless and often boring activities—what do you do? I'll tell you. Go to him whose church it is! The fruitfulness of the church is his glory. He is far more concerned for its welfare than you are. But be forewarned: prayer for God's renewing can shake things up a bit. God can often cause a convulsion by bringing problems to the surface. We need only read the accounts of the great revivals of the church to see this.

Often, however, as subversive transformers we do not know where to begin or what the problem is. We confront humanly insurmountable obstacles, absolute inertia, decades of lifeless tradition, merely human agendas, and sometimes an almost malignant hostility to any suggestion that anything should be different. What do we do? Where do we begin?

Or, again, something among us hinders the refreshing, life-giving rain of God's blessing. Everything on the surface looks proper, but deadness prevails and the Spirit is quenched. How do you get to the heart of the problem? What will it take to find out what the deadening element is? Where is it? Where is the "accursed thing" that brings defeat to the armies of Israel?

God knows. He sees. He is able to cleanse and renew. The church is his, and he waits to be asked. So we must pray.

In one of the great episodes of revival in the Christian church, in the Hebrides off the coast of Scotland, the only apparent cause for the radical transformation of life and morals that took place under the preaching of some ordinary Christians was the faithful, daily prayer of a small group.

The common denominator among every congregation which experiences real transformation (in distinction from some humanly contrived "success" program) is prayer. There is always a group of persons earnestly praying and asking God *to do what he must do* to bring cleansing, quickening and fruitfulness to the congregation. Prayer reaches beyond human limitations and brings God into the process.

I must confess that I am always restive with the purveyors of church renewal formulas who tell you how to do everything to organize your church for renewal but never mention prayer. Not that the suggestions, wisdom and techniques offered are wrong. Rather, without God's blessing and the enabling of the Holy Spirit, they are fruitless and frustrating and produce merely human results.

We have only to look at the example of our Lord Jesus and his apostles to realize what a prominent place they gave to prayer. The fountain of blessing is not human ingenuity, or energy or good intentions, but the Lord himself. He alone is the source of the rivers of living water which make the desert blossom like a rose.

Prayer—An Expression of Faith

Prayer expresses our confidence in God. Through it we offer our worship, our praise, our heartfelt thanks. Prayer is the Christian and the Christian community coming to the eternal God, who has bidden us to address him with the affectionate familial word *Fa-*

ther. And as we come to him we acknowledge that his name, and the honor of his name, is the church's ultimate desire.

When we pray we take God seriously. And because we take him seriously, we also take his Word seriously. Thus when the Christian community (whether the whole congregation or the smaller church within the church) studies the Scriptures, it does so in prayer. We meditate on his Word so that it will bear fruit in and among us.

Mindless prayer is not the norm for the Christian community. Jesus warned us against the use of vain repetitions and empty-sounding phrases just in order to make others think we are praying and pious. When Paul was instructing the Christians at Corinth about the use of ecstatic tongues in prayer, he didn't deny their place in prayer, but he did insist that Christians pray with the *understanding* also.

When speaking of prayer as an expression of faith, then, what I want to indicate is that in church renewal we must begin by getting to know from our study of Scripture who God is and what his will is. We then offer that understanding and ourselves back to him in prayer. We ask for a transformation of our congregation (and the church beyond) that accords with his kingdom purposes, knowing that such prayer is an expression of our confidence in who God is.

Scripture which is not meditated on, prayed over and applied is not really known. Only in prayer does our understanding become existential for us.

The God who reveals himself also calls us to faith and gives us prayer as an expression of that faith. God and his name become the focus of our lives and the motivation for church renewal. To overlook this discipline is disastrous. Horace Fenton's "sure-fire formula for evading missionary responsibility" applies equally well to undermining redemptive subversion: (1) consider the immensity of the task, (2) look at the meagerness of your resources and (3) leave God out!

Prayer is the expression of our faith in God, and of his unsearchable riches and resources which are available to us as his subversives.

Faith—Commitment to Truth

Faith involves our commitment to the *truth* as it is made known in Jesus Christ and recorded in Holy Scripture. Our faith rests on the joyous announcement of the kingdom of God drawn nigh in the person of Jesus of Nazareth. It is directed toward the focus and content of the gospel. The Christian community is not agnostic or neutral or indifferent to the truth. Jesus identified himself with the truth when he said: "If you continue in my word, you are my disciples, and you will know the truth, and the truth will make you free" (Jn 8:31-32 RSV). And, "I am the way and the truth and the life" (Jn 14:6 NIV).

We are not talking here about some sterile, theological orthodoxy, some scriptural proposition held impersonally. The faith that renews the person and renews the church is that joyous, thrilled trust in Jesus as he is set forth in Scripture. It is this truth that captivates mind and will and produces contagious new life. Scripture is the Word of the Father, Son and Holy Spirit. It evangelizes, cleanses, informs, sets free and equips us for every good work.

Because the Christian community needs a soil rich in faith, we need to look for ways to plow generous portions of faith into the life of the community—and keep on doing it. It is this truth, this faith, that produces freedom. It protects from error. It nurtures into maturity.

Jesus told his own to go and make disciples, "teaching them to observe all that I have commanded you" (Mt 28:20 RSV). Paul wrote to the Christians at Rome that he wanted to come and evangelize them again (Rom 1:15). The church always needs evangelizing to be reminded of and thrilled afresh with the wonder of what God has done in Jesus Christ. Pope John Paul I, the short-lived pope, said in an address that the major task confronting the church today was to evangelize those already baptized. This is even more true when the knowledge and awareness of the gospel have faded and the darkness has reasserted itself.

So how do we begin to cultivate faith within the church? Where are the handles? Peter told the Christians in dispersion that they should be completely devoted to Christ in their hearts and then be ready to give to any person who asked them a reason for their hope in Christ (1 Pet 3:15)—and that's not a bad place to start.

At a rather critical moment in our congregation, some years back, God brought into our midst a family who, would you believe, had been converted to Christ while they were serving as missionaries. They had come home for some graduate studies in a nearby university and identified with our church.

Now if you think they weren't a faith-creating factor, then you need to think again! In conversation after conversation they lovingly and pointedly shared with others the difference between being a well-intentioned church member and being a disciple of Jesus Christ. What they demonstrated again and again is the value of *one-on-one conversations* in cultivating faith. Such conversations should be as natural as breathing.

And, *knife-and-fork hospitality* is as old as the New Testament records and as fresh as today. The dining-room table is a warm place to invite friends and to share with them our involvement with Jesus Christ. Taking a friend home for lunch doesn't require enormous preparations, yet it is a valuable strategy for finding fellow adventurers who would like to join you in the ministry of church transformation. A lot of Bible-study groups have been born over a cup of coffee. Just last Sunday a couple of friends invited us over for peanut butter and tomato sandwiches (I recognize that the cuisine might differ from your tastes!), and we cooked up a discussion on ways to minister to the church that you wouldn't believe.

Such informal gatherings can lead to a *home Bible study,* when one Christian meets another and they agree to spend time togeth er reading and discussing Scripture in order to nurture their faith This energizes faith and has been a key element in the transfor mation of more congregations that one can number. Similar, but with a little more structure and commitment is the *house church or covenant group*. The difference is that in these a group, of whatever size, commit themselves to each other to be a caring, learning, praying, ministering fellowship for a given period of time.

I was in such a covenant group a few years ago. It was a delight. We called it Kelly's Bible Study after a red Irish setter named Kelly, who always seemed to enjoy all of those extra people in his house and put on something of a show. What happened around Kelly, though, had an impact on all of our lives and the church. In addition to studying Scripture, praying together in smaller cells and occasionally meeting around the Lord's Table, we periodically read through some book that assisted us in our quest for deeper discipleship. The contagion of this group wholesomely infected the larger congregation and continues to do so.

Historically, it was the class meetings that were at the heart of the Wesleyan revivals. John Wesley had the good wisdom to have all of the converts in small nurture and accountability groups. It is covenant groups such as these, called *base communities*, that are at the heart of the vigor of much of the awakening in Latin America today. And in one of the largest congregations in the world—in Seoul, South Korea—that church's structuring into neighborhood house churches is credited with giving it its enormous vitality.

Put this high on your agenda as a redemptive subversive.

Most congregations are looking for teachers for a church-school class—so recognize *church-school classes* as a prime opportunity for faith cultivation. Our friend Ann was a vivacious product of the Jesus Revolution who came bouncing into our congregation with zeal and verve and looking for a place to minister. She chose one of those tired, old traditional adult Sunday-school classes that had existed forever! Her dynamic and loving faith and affection for those older folk was absolutely transforming, and seasons of refreshing came into an unlikely spot.

Whenever you have the opportunity to *teach and expound Scrip-*

ture, you have a choice occasion to enrich the soil of the fellowship. Most congregations, even those with somewhat evangelical reputations, are prone to be biblically illiterate. If you happen to be the pastor, then you have the opportunity to teach Scripture every Sunday. But if you do it, then do it as a skilled steward of God's Word. It is reported that William Orange in New Zealand, by patient teaching of Scripture to a boy's weekday class and through exposition at morning and evening prayers in his Anglican parish, transformed the whole diocese in his lifetime and sent scores into pastoral and missionary service. I have the hunch that most of the good Bible teaching in the church is done by conscientious laypersons who equip others in a knowledge of Scripture.

And don't forget *the value of literature* in cultivating faith within the congregation. I have a couple of friends who are forever finding good literature and passing it on to other friends, who then read it and pass it to somebody else. We are a generation blessed with a lot of good and inexpensive Christian literature (and, alas, some not so good). Every year I find some good book that helps me in my understanding of living churches and dynamic faith, and I make it required reading for our church's leadership team. Year by year I see those ideas taking root and producing good fruit among us. It is surprising how good literature can get into the bloodstream of a congregation.

These are starting places.

Before we move on, though, we need to remind ourselves that the purpose of faith is not just to *know* it, but to *do* it. Faith grows as faith obeys. The man who built his house upon the rock was the man who received the word and did it. Also, we don't use truth as a weapon with which to assault others. The truth is to be spoken in love and with gentleness.

And so we come to love and hope, which are the topics of the next chapter.

7
Redemptive Subversion: Love & Hope

She was a stranger to me. She had asked me for an appointment. She came in, sat down and said, "Let me get right to the point. I have been attending church all of my life, and it has been pretty sterile. I visited your church for several Sundays, and that is what I want to talk to you about. There is something going on here. Your people love each other. Tell me what's going on. I've never experienced this kind of love before."

Now isn't that a happy word?

This was after about seven years of struggle in the Pioneer Plunge through "many a conflict and many a doubt." But it was the harbinger of a new day of God's blessing on the redemptive subversion by a faithful cadre of transformers among us.

In Paul's fathomless hymn to love (1 Cor 13) he states that among the triad of faith, hope and love, love is the greatest. In the letter to the Christians at Colossae he says that love binds all else together in perfect harmony (Col 3:14).

And what is love? Love is God's liberating and recreating purpose toward persons. If faith involves a commitment to truth, then love involves a commitment to persons. Love takes persons seriously—as seriously as God does in Christ. A congregation that is not the embodiment of love is inimical to the gospel. Sin produces estrangement, alienation and indifference to other persons. Lack of love is the essence of sin and produces insensitivity, unrighteousness, manipulation, oppression and trivialization.

Love is not to be hokey or unlistening or merely verbal. It isn't meant to be just "spiritual." Love should be genuine, practical, tough and costly. Love keeps the other person (even "enemies") in view. Love has to do with relationships, with the quality of interpersonal life within the Christian community. We love because God first loved us. O, how he loved us! So, as Paul states it: "The love of God leaves us no choice" (2 Cor 5:14 NEB).

In a nutshell, love gives and doesn't demand response or repayment.

In studying the ministry of redemptive subversion, we need to read and re-read 1 Corinthians 13. It rebukes all of our spiritual elitism and calls us to the ministry of practical and enduring love. That kind of love must begin with God at work in you and me. As we are loved by God, then we are set free to begin to be agents of love within our congregations.

Look at your congregation, and see how very much it needs someone to take others seriously and sensitively, to listen and to be a redemptive force in relationships. Love is not just toward "our kind of folks" or "nice people." Remember, that when *we* were helpless, ungodly sinners and enemies (Rom 5:6-11) God loved us. We all look for that kind of unconditional love, though such ministry can be taxing, frustrating, draining and costly. So be it!

While we are speaking primarily of the ministry of love within the congregation, the love of Christ in us is *not turned exclusively inward.* The very passage quoted from Romans reminds us that when we were *outside* of Christ, he died to bring us in. Jesus was the friend of sinners, and the church, his people, needs to have that reputation also. He said that it was not those who were well that needed a physician, but those who were sick—so he came to seek and to save the lost.

Those persons around us who are morally, spiritually, physically, or demonically sick and oppressed must also be the objects of our love. Whenever a congregation becomes too comfortable and too devoid of really needy persons, then some yellow lights ought to go on in our corporate thinking, in our hearts. General William Booth, Mother Teresa of Calcutta and countless others remind us that the church is to be a demonstration of God's love to the outcasts of this world, to the "nobodies" of our society.

Jesus said that by our love the world would know that we were his disciples. So then if the hallmark of the Christian community is love, how do we get it richly into the mix?

Prayer—the First Act of Love

As we pray for God's will to be done, we immediately are faced with the implications of that prayer for ourselves. Jesus taught us that if we loved him, we would then keep his commandments. In love, then, we offer ourselves in obedience to our Lord Jesus whenever we pray for his will to be done. We make ourselves available to be instruments of love in prayer.

I cannot count the times that I have been bent out of shape with the fellowship or with somebody in it and discovered as I went to prayer before God that the problem was within me—with my pride, my selfish agenda, my impatience. So by the time I got through praying, I was already at peace with God, and the problem had essentially been solved.

I begin loving by praying for the other person. Jesus began his ministry in prayer. Before every major decision and episode in his ministry he came and offered himself anew to the Father. He prayed for his disciples. He prayed for those who would later believe on him.

But as we see in the Lord's Prayer, it is not enough that we pray for others and for the forgiveness of our own sins. We must be prepared to forgive others their sins as well. The restoring of the relationship between two who are estranged over some issue is of such import to God that Jesus says it is linked to their relationship with God as well: "For if you forgive men when they sin against you, your heavenly Father will also forgive you. But if you do not forgive men their sins, your Father will not forgive your sins" (Mt 6:14-15 NIV).

A community of love begins in prayer. I pray for you. You pray for me. We pray for each other. When there are differences and barriers and alienation and indifference among us, then we begin the reconciliation by praying for each other. A conflict within the community should turn on our yellow lights and call us to prayer. We ask God to pour out his love into our hearts according to the word of promise (Rom 5:5).

Prayer as the first act of love, bears the community of faith up to God just as the Old Testament priest wore the names of the tribes of Israel upon his breastplate when he went into the holy of holies. Even so, as a redemptive subversive I begin my caring by praying for the brothers and sisters whom God has given me in this family. I pray for my enemies, and for those difficult persons in the community who are also part of the family of God. In love we pray away the barriers.

In prayer I ask that my own love be refined and made genuine. I deliberately ask that my own selfishness and petulance and obtuseness and insensitivity be made obvious so that I can confess it, repent of it, put it to death and be made free to love others as Christ has loved me.

I pray also for that kind of "Jubilee love" that looks on the naked and hungry and thirsty and sick and imprisoned with practical and redemptive compassion, for if that is not part of my love, then my love is not authentic (Mt 25:31-46).

Prayer is the first act of love.

Cultivating Love in the Church
Start developing love by being a lover! And start being a lover by taking time to listen to and get to know other persons. A basic flaw in relationally sterile Christian communities is that not enough time is spent to create the kind of dialog needed to listen to one another, seek understanding, ask questions, get inside another's

skin and thus come to appreciate one another as real persons. Frequently, instead, we preach, teach, witness, pray, tell what we think and criticize—all without ever really knowing one another, never really taking others seriously.

During a break in a Bible class made very sticky by Jerry's domination and obvious insecurity, Earl went over to him and asked, "Jerry, at some point in your life you met Jesus and made a decision to believe him and follow him, which has brought you to this moment. I'd love to hear about it!" And the floodgates opened. There were tears, there was a rehearsing of earlier painful days, and the decision for Christ, and when the Bible class resumed, it was not the same. Love takes time to listen and to know.

Love is an open home and an open table. Hospitality is a ministry of love. It is also one of the most mentioned gifts of the Holy Spirit. I can never get over the change in chemistry when people come into our home. These are the same people I have met in the church building, but it is different at home. I'm sometimes glad we have church buildings, but then I'm not always sure that the advent of church buildings was a blessing.

The early church was not burdened with them. The church gathered in homes, which meant that they weren't dealing with huge and impersonal crowds. Common meals were shared. Homes were refuges for strangers and for the hurting. They were places of warmth for the friendless. They were a place to sleep for the homeless and a gesture of friendship to the lonely. So it could and should be today—except that we too often make our homes a place of privacy for ourselves and then send folks off to restaurants or to the Salvation Army. Not so in the New Testament. An open home, however simple, is a tangible expression of love.

A place to start in cultivating love is to begin inviting folks from your congregation into your home or apartment for a snack, for conversation and an occasion to get to know them as persons. Make your dinner table a place of ministry. Not gourmet episodes, unless that is your thing, but a setting of loving care and availability. In most congregations that I know of there are more lonely and hurting persons, more "strangers" than you can imagine.

By making your home, your apartment, your quarters a model of hospitality and of love, you can really cultivate love in the community. It will cost you, but redemptive subversion makes this a major ministry.

Love doesn't consider its possessions as its own. Love has economic dimensions. We live in a society obsessed with financial security. Yet, if I read my New Testament correctly one of the more prominent evidences of love in the fresh new church in Jerusalem was that no one considered anything that he owned as his own. There is a "kingdom economy" revealed here. Love doesn't accumulate, rather it gives away.

This flies in the face of all we are conditioned to believe in our consumer-oriented, upwardly mobile, *Wall Street Journal* culture. But the Old Testament Torah, the prophets, the Gospels, and the apostolic teachings all concur that what we possess is not our own. Probably one of the most untouchable bastions of our lovelessness and self-indulgence in the Christian church is in our possessions, our property.

Unfortunately, even as the Old Testament community seemed to forget and relegate to obscurity the wonderful Jubilee observance, today you find the Christian church forgetting this dimension of its ministry of love. There is marvelous old Barnabas in the book of Acts, selling, giving and encouraging, and he has his offspring in the contemporary church, though one could wish his example were more frequently emulated. There are those such as Millard Fuller, who divested himself of wealth and a dazzling business career to start Habitat for Humanity, which provides low-cost homes for the poor around the world as a Christian ministry and witness. There are undoubtedly many others doing the same in obscurity and humility. And we need to revive it in ourselves and in our churches. It is evidently a very common witness in third world churches. May it become so in ours.

Love is being a flower growing in a manure pile. Jesus taught us to pray, "Deliver us from evil," and, sure enough, one of the realities we face in being redemptive subversives is that within the church there are all kinds of evidences that the Prince of Darkness has brought his discouraging, destructive, deceiving efforts to bear.

Sometimes the church looks much more like the kingdom of darkness than it does like the kingdom of light. There is a whole lot that stinks inside the church. Endless, meaningless clutter often obscures the purpose and mission of the church. There are not a few neurotic personalities. And those who hurl fiery darts are not some bizarre minions invented by Steven Spielberg, but too often the pillars of the church in three-piece suits.

One of the first times I came nose to nose with the pain of such an encounter was when I was young and innocent and envisoned that everyone was basically good and well-intentioned. And then I ran into Mr. Durwaite, who was the most outspoken elder in the church and whose wife was the self-appointed queen mother of the women of the church. He was just plain mean! He never had a positive proposal. He was devious and untruthful and brought a cloud of miasmic discouragement everywhere he went. Oh, he had a pious mouth. "What can we do to improve our church?" was his standard response to anyone who questioned him.

Adventurers in the church must not get cynical about this. It is part of the spiritual conflict in this between-the-ages Christian community of which we are a part. And the role of love is to stand in positive, beautiful, sweet-smelling contrast to the evidences of darkness that may be all around. And you can be sure that probably most of the congregation are really quiet and hopeful Christians who long for God's transforming grace just as you do.

Because there always have been, are, and will continue to be differences and conflicts in the family of God, *love is a reconciler.* Love is a resolver of conflicts, and this is about as practical a ministry as you can have. At the very least, love is able to discuss even the most serious disagreements in love. That other person's point of view is not unimportant, especially if love is a commitment to persons. In Ephesians Paul speaks of the church as the fulfillment of God's purpose in which all things are brought together, where barriers come down, and where we in the church become one. Love, then, begins with us, and begins where there are those things that divide.

Strange as it may seem, we as agents of love ought to have a keen eye for those expressions of face or body that indicate difference, pain, division or lurking conflict. In Ephesians it appears to be social, racial, class and cultural boundaries that are in view. In other settings it could be political or economic. Usually, in most moribund congregations, it is something of no consequence at all, such as the choice of wallpaper in the ladies' bathroom!

Jesus taught us that if we have something against our brother or sister, we are to go and get it settled right away before we ever come to the altar to worship. Love is being willing to confess my part in hurting my brothers and sisters or in my complicity in disillusioning other members of the fellowship. But love is also forgiving. I confess my own sin, but I am ready to forgive those who have done me in.

Have you noticed how frequently that rather than exercise this basic teaching of Jesus and the apostles, folks will simply move their membership to another congregation?

Love doesn't go looking for trouble or spoiling for a fight. Quite the contrary, love goes to the heart of differences that estrange, and works through them with gentleness, sensitivity, patience and forthrightness. In our own fellowship we are always alerted when there is a minority vote in our leadership team for this very reason. It can indicate that there may be some estrangement there that needs to be brought to the surface. More than that, it may be that the Holy Spirit is checking the majority through that minority voice. Love has the readiness to stop and work through that difference. Christ has given us the ministry of reconciliation, and that's practical!

Love also submits lovingly and willingly to oversight and accountability. In most sick congregations there is a very negative response to the legitimate leadership of the church. Something about our unregenerate nature, our flesh, has a very difficult time being submissive to anybody.

It is true that church leaders are to be models of love, as well as faith and hope. And if that leadership degenerates into the loveless exercise of power, then that leadership becomes a pathology and not a blessing. But I want to focus on the other end of that relationship.

Those who want to be redemptive subversives in their congregation need to learn the ministry of love, and the submission in love, to the legitimate, duly ordained leadership of the fellowship. Human leadership is always human, always imperfect—and yet it is God-ordained. To criticize, to snipe at and to undermine that leadership is not a ministry of love. It is destructive and makes the critic part of the pathology.

But to encourage, to pray for, to communicate with, to love and supportively relate to those persons who are leaders is a beautiful ministry of love (Heb 13:7-8, 17).

I can recall when a group of folk in a very tense time covenanted to pray regularly for God's grace on our leadership team. The leadership was under severe criticism because of a very difficult decision they had had to make, and those dear intercessors in love began to uphold and encourage the leaders with prayers. What a tangible difference it made! For anyone dedicated to being a redemptive subversive, I cannot think of a more fruitful ministry. I mean, face it, sometimes leaders may not even be Christians, but they are still the duly ordained leaders and deserving of the brotherly support of love.

And that's practical.

Let me tell you a story, which was told to me by Bill Iverson. It is the story of a mother and a child during the tense racial riots in Newark, New Jersey, in the late sixties. Outside were all the sounds of sirens, explosions, shouts and the urban agony of that era. The mother and child were in an apartment several floors up, frightened by all that was happening. Periodically the child would begin to cry, and the mother would rock her and say, "Hush, child, it's all right. God is with us." This worked a few times, but finally the child couldn't handle that any longer, and said, "I don't want God. I want somebody with skin on!"

She wanted some help she could see and touch and talk to. Ministering love in your congregation is being love with skin on. It is being God's agent of love to the real persons who need to be related in love to him. This becomes your ministry. Love is present. It builds up. It cares. It is patient. It is a servant. It is genuine. It can rebuke and reprove because it cares. It is not reactive or irritable or resentful. We can love so because we are so loved.

People don't know we're Christians because of our orthodoxy and pure doctrine. They know we are Christ's disciples because we love each other as he loves us.

The health and life, the beauty and joyous fulfillment found in a congregation where love abounds constitute that state of blessedness which the Father intends for his family. But neither faith nor love is sufficient without the other, nor are they together sufficient without hope. It is the combination of all three that produces kingdom-shaped churches.

Hope—a Commitment to God's Sovereign Purpose

The New Testament abounds with such excited themes as the new aeon, the new creation, God's future invading our present, the age to come, and other such concepts fraught with the anticipation of God's good purpose. It is that sense of anticipation, that note of hope, that is missing in the congregational soil of so many sterile churches. It is lacking in churches that are only concerned with their own survival, churches that can revel in their past but have no sense of future.

Betty and I visited a lovely Episcopal church in low country South Carolina one Easter Sunday. It fairly reeked of antebellum South—moss-draped trees around the cemetery, headstones dating back to the Revolutionary War. Inside, the church was an episode in history and in the architecture of that period. Around the walls were marble markers commemorating Civil War heroes and the departed saints who had served in government and the military.

Frankly, I am a history buff, and I think it is good and necessary to celebrate our heritage and our past as a congregation. But, when a church only has eyes for the past, or even only for the present, then it is in trouble! When it takes for its motto the words "As it was in the beginning, is now, and ever shall be"—then it has succumbed to hopelessness. Many congregations have fallen victims to that pathology.

A congregation hesitates, a neighborhood changes, a prominent member dies, a gifted leader moves away, and people begin looking backward. They begin reminiscing about the good old days, and the congregation fades into hopelessness. Yet right in the same neighborhood another congregation, perhaps with less real human assets, is prospering and reaching out.

This happened a few years ago in Newark, New Jersey. An old established congregation dwindled down to so few members that they put their building up for sale. Face it, Newark is an urban wilderness if there ever was one. Yet in this same neighborhood was a young vibrant congregation that was started from scratch in the late 1940s and that lived redemptively with the realities of that city. They had engaged in tough evangelism, winning and nurturing people from the highways and hedges of that mixed ethnic community. As they grew they had a vision of winning Newark to Christ, and of every member being part of that missionary task in that vast and complicated urban wasteland. When the older congregation put its building up for sale, the Calvary Gospel Church bought it and proceeded to add to it a Christian school and to engage in many satellite ministries that have been a paradigm of urban Christian outreach.

We had to face a quite similar situation in our congregation in Durham. The church had been established to minister to the textile community that had grown up around a local mill. In time a university surrounded the mill village, and the mill housing was sold off and the neighborhood was essentially dismantled. We had to stop and look at where we had come from, but then, more important, at what God wanted us to do in the future. It was then that we realized that our new ministry should be to the "poor benighted aborigines" in the university and to a coming generation of young adults moving into the apartment complexes nearby.

The difference between a dying congregation and one throbbing with life is the element of hope.

So any living congregation needs to have a generous portion of hope in its fertile soil. If faith is a commitment to truth, and love is a commitment to persons, then *hope is a commitment to the sovereign purpose of God in Jesus Christ.* Hope is a movement from despair and resignation to the consummation of all things at the coming of Jesus Christ. Hope is a movement from things as they are, to the God who in Christ created all things new. Hope is the outworking of Easter in the life of the church.

Jesus is risen and alive. Nothing is "locked in" any longer.[1] All things are possible. Resurrection power is unleashed in the world through the church. Hope looks right into the face of the demonic and Satanic and hears "I will build my church and the gates of death and hell shall not prevail against it."

Hope sings "This is my father's world: O let me ne'er forget that though the wrong seems oft so strong, God is the ruler yet." Hope is the saints beneath the altar in heaven crying "O Sovereign Lord, holy and true, how long before thou wilt judge and avenge our blood?" and knowing that God will surely do it. Hope sees beyond the temporal to the eternal.

Hope is Advent. Hope is Easter. Hope is Pentecost. Hope strains against the impossible, reaches beyond faith and stretches beyond its experience. Hope makes the most humanly impossible barriers the occasion for breathless expectation as it looks to God. It is this that makes hope a *sine qua non* of the church, especially for redemptive subversives.

Hope knows that where sin abounds, grace shall much more

abound (Rom 6:20). So no matter how dark the night in a cultural context, the church knows that God intends to bring the light into that very night. Hope gives to the Christian community its sense of meaning, of history, of destiny. Hope liberates us from the confines of the present and the past, and moves us out into God's future!

From a purely human point of view, if we thought ourselves to be terminally ill and without any possible cure, we would be hopeless and thus resigned to death. Yet, if our physician were to tell us that a cure had been discovered and tested and proven effective, even though we ourselves had not experienced it yet, hope would dawn. Then, were the new cure applied to us and we were to begin to experience the first evidences of restored health, we would then long for the consummation of the cure, for full health. We, then, who were once without hope, would now live in eager anticipation.[2]

So also we, who were once without hope, have received the good news of Jesus Christ first of all in the announcement of truth and love and all of the promises of God in Christ. Hope dawned and we embraced Christ by faith. Then, in the Christian community that faith and love were experienced a bit more. The power of God and the grace of God were experienced, perhaps only faintly, perhaps only at the Eucharist and the promise of more. And hope grew, and with it the eager desire to experience the fullness of faith and love in Jesus Christ.

As we behold lives changed and prayers answered, as obstacles are overcome and the blessings of the Lord are evidenced, the anticipation grows as to what it must be like to know his love and his being fully. That hope, then, motivates us to new obedience and to new devotion and to new zeal. Hope bears us through the dark night of the soul and through the deep waters of human tragedy.

The church must also have such hopeful perspective. After all, we are more than conquerors through him who loved us (Rom 8:37).

Prayer—the Language of Hope

The writer of the letter to the Hebrews says that faith is the assurance of things hoped for, the conviction of things not seen (Heb 11:1). We pray for what we know is the will of God for his church, and in so doing we pray for what we cannot yet see. We look at the kingdom-shaped community, which we explored in chapter five, and we pray that these God-ordained visions shall become realities in our own Pioneer Plunge.

Paul writes: "For in this hope we were saved. Now hope that is seen is not hope. For who hopes for what he sees? But if we hope for what we do not see, we wait for it with patience" (Rom 8:24-25 RSV).

We know that God wants his people to dwell in the fullness of his Spirit, and that he wants the church to be a community of love that is genuine and practical. We know that God wants his people to reach out to the poor and the oppressed and the fractured who are living around us. He wants us to bring hope to the helpless poor. He wants us to use our own wealth as kingdom citizens and with kingdom priorities. He wants to deliver us from our idolatry to wealth and power. He wants to powerfully change our lives. We know that God wants the power structures of this age to see in the church the manifold wisdom of God (Eph 3:10). We know all of these things and more . . . yet we so seldom see even the first glimpse of this in reality.

Is it fantasy to think that such things can be true right here in the First Church of River City? Or do we resign ourselves to the dismal prospect that our congregation is more than even God can handle?

Of course we don't. We express our valid hope in prayer to the God "who by the power at work within us is able to do far more abundantly than all that we ask or think" (Eph 3:20 RSV).

Hallelujah! God is able to do far more than we can even think. He wills to be glorified in his church, and *that's us!* What do we do? We flee to him in prayer, and in the strong name of Jesus Christ we pray for that power to transform this barren congregation—its membership, its traditions, its mentality—into an instrument of praise.

That's hope.

The church is in continual conflict. We live between the ages. We live in the presence of both the kingdom of darkness and the kingdom of light. On the one hand all of the principalities and powers, all of the intangible influences of evil and unrighteousness and destruction are the context of our Christian pilgrimage. On the other hand we live as citizens of the kingdom of God which has been inaugurated at the coming of our Lord Jesus but which has not yet been consummated, though it will be at his return at the end of the age.

This means that the church must ever be aware of this conflict. The church is a sign of the age to come. It is the community of the kingdom of God. We know, therefore, that the forces of Satan and of darkness are always seeking to destroy the church, though they shall not prevail. The clash of the kingdoms of darkness and of light is keenly felt by the Christian community. The clash is often political or economic and not infrequently, as with Jesus, religious.

Our adversary, the devil, is a crafty foe, and his machinations to discourage, to erode, to misdirect the church are clever and subtle. We know this. We are told by our Lord Jesus that the world hates us because we belong to him. We keep trying to forget this word or to ignore it, or to make it not so. But it remains true. We sing of it in S. J. Stone's hymn *The Church's One Foundation:*

Though with a scornful wonder
Men see us sore oppressed,
By schisms rent asunder,
By heresies distressed:
Yet saints their watch are keeping,
Their cry goes up, "How long?"
And soon the night of weeping
Shall be the morn of song.

Conflict and hope. Yet hope knows that the victory belongs to the

Lord, and so it prays. Prayer is the language of hope.

You create an atmosphere, a climate of healthy expectation and readiness in your congregational family by prayer. Blessing begins with the very act of prayer. In your devotions, in your class, in your Bible study group and in your services of worship, *pray!* Open yourself to the wondrous working of God, to his cleansing, to his preparation, to his creativity, to confession and repentance, to new obedience, to praise and adoration and thanksgiving. "Not to want to pray," said P. T. Forsyth, "is the sin behind sin."[3]

Cultivating Hope in the Church

How to enrich the church with the element of hope is a bit more difficult. Hope is an attitude, not an activity or a discipline. In practical affairs it is the community of Christians looking beyond the present, dreaming dreams and seeing visions. Lloyd Ogilvie has made familiar a set of questions which all redemptive subversives need to keep in mind:

a. What kind of Christians do you wish your church to turn out into your community and the world?

b. What kind of congregation produces that kind of Christian?

c. What kind of leadership produces that kind of congregation?

Jerry Kirk asks a visionary question too: If you had no fear of failure, what would you and your congregation attempt for God?

Perhaps your role in the transformation of your congregation is to keep asking questions like these of your friends and congregational leaders.

Recently a new brother joined our congregation. In the initial meeting with the elders he asked the question: "Tell me, where is this church going? What do you see as your future? What do you think God wants to accomplish through you and me?"

Happily, one of our elders was able to give him a crisp answer because we had just spent time working this over at a weekend retreat. That retreat is an annual time in which we pray, dream, do creative thinking about our future ministry as a congregation, and define the steps needed to achieve those dreams.

If no one else seems to be dreaming dreams and generating hope, then you at least must be one who does. Then others will join you in that ministry. In business, companies are always projecting five- and ten-year plans, always doing marketing surveys, always attempting to meet the future. The New Testament also requires that we look beyond our immediate problems and obstacles to see God's ultimate purpose in the consummation of all things at the coming of our Lord Jesus Christ.

Don't forget hope. Leave out any one of the three—faith, love, hope—and you will have a critical imbalance. But with these, no matter how hostile the environment, the kingdom-shaped church we are seeking will begin to emerge. Engage in these three ministries well and patiently. This is the irreducible beginning of the renewal of the church. These efforts are not merely human. And when you engage in them, you are not on your own. The Spirit of God is at work in you and through you. So take heart!

Postscript

You may wonder what you are looking for by way of fruit of your ministry as a redemptive subversive. As you cultivate faith and love and hope into your present congregational family, what will begin to sprout? Let me answer that by harking back to the signs of the kingdom mentioned in chapter five:

1. A clear grasp on the apostolic faith of Jesus Christ.
2. True and lively worship of the triune God.
3. Loving service to one another and to humankind.
4. Healthy and bold witness in word and deed.
5. Loving and practical fellowship and interdependence among the community of believers.

In your ministry of transformation, keep an eye out for these evidences of the kingdom, and give thanks.

May God give you an extravagant anointing of faith and love and hope—and a hearty sense of humor! The Lord be with you.

8
Beyond Membership to Ministry

We began this adventure together using a lot of ir-reverent designations for your church and mine. We spoke of survival in the church, of Shammah in the beanpatch. We talked of Pioneer Plunges and of Nineveh congregations. Our design is now obvious. We are looking at a very holy calling to the ministry of church renewal, and this ministry belongs to us all.

Our calling to be saints, to be lights in the dark world, to be persons who walk in the Spirit—all of this speaks of the calling to be agents of God's new creation. That calling is always dynamic and always incomplete. And it is always an adventure. As God's garden by neglect reverts to wilderness, as the community of the light by indifference succumbs to the darkness, then we are called to be part of the ministry of restoration and renewal.

The wilderness theme is a rich one in biblical studies. In a time of deep personal agony and the dark night of the soul, I was studying the opening chapters of the gospel of Mark and came across both John the Baptist and Jesus meeting God in the wilderness. A footnote pointed me to the fact that after the Exodus God had met Israel in the wilderness as he had met Moses there before. And down through the centuries that wilderness theme emerges as the place where God meets his people and brings fresh calling and blessing.

What we have been rehearsing here is that many congregations have become wildernesses, devoid of joy, of gospel, of life and light. Humanly speaking, they can bring us to despair—or they can become for us that place where, away from all human confidences, you and I are brought to a fresh meeting with God and we hear his calling to become his ministers of new creation. And that is a calling to high adventure replete with dangers and ecstasy.

That surely has been the case in the several chapters of my pilgrimage in the church. I come to a new congregation and groan at the wilderness. Then, after getting over my own whimpering self-pity, I find that God meets me there and assures me that I am there for his purposes. I have never known where that calling would carry me. The congregations surely were not aware that there was such a subversive among them. But slowly it has dawned on my sluggish heart that God never intends for his people to be the hapless victims of churches reverting to darkness, and he surely does not intend for us to be passive.

He calls us rather to be dynamic, working agents in his glorious purpose of bringing those same congregations back to their sense of calling as kingdom communities. This is the ministry of church renewal. It is evidence of the wilderness within us that we so often fail to grasp the wonder of God's gifts and calling in us. The consequence is that we have little sense of the transcendent in the midst of the humiliation of our daily incarnation in the wilderness. Yet God meets with his people time and again in the wilderness in order to confirm his transcendent purpose for their lives

That realization has put thrills into my daily existence. Just to realize that God has called me and prepared me to be a dynamic part of his purpose puts a whole new face on the mundane. It gives fresh meaning to Paul's teaching that we hold the treasure of God in clay pots so that the transcendent glory may belong to God and not to us (2 Cor 4:7).

Jesus has taught us that just as the Father sent him, so he sends us (Jn 20:21). And with that awesome commission he bestows the breath of God upon us to empower us. Jesus was sent to be the incarnation, the flesh-and-blood instrument of the Father—and so are we. This calling and sending has both personal and corporate dimensions. It is a task given to us individually as persons and corporately as the church. That task, or commission, is to demonstrate God's heart and mind in the midst of humankind. We are to be a demonstration of the gospel of the kingdom. We are to be conformed to the likeness of the Son of God (Rom 8:29).

For the moment set aside all of the grandiose and triumphal ideas you might have. Set aside also the notions of prominence that too often accompany our teachings of ministry. It is distressing that many who are zealous for renewal in congregations cling to such aspirations, so much so that they feel slighted or persecuted if they are not chosen right away to teach or to lead.

Calling to the ministry of renewal begins with the freedom to be a servant! It is a calling to be a gentle, sensitive, loving, caring and joyous instrument of the gospel. It begins with being that source of living waters in the quiet one-on-one service of encouragement.

A dear and faithful friend, who is to me a paradigm of the ministry of renewal, told me of his beginning in a congregation that was nothing but discouragement and arridity. He said that all he could resolve to do was to be a "genuine Christian brother"! He related to me that in the congregation he had never heard anyone speak of any Christian whom they really admired, if indeed they even knew what a Christian was. His covenant with God was to quietly model true Christian faith and life in the midst of the congregation. He was, in fact, the instrument of an awakening that transformed that congregation. What he did, for the most part, is what I have suggested in these pages, namely, he became an expression of faith, love and hope. He nurtured the "bruised reed and the smoking flax," those weak beginnings in the lives of others. He was the catalyst for a weekly prayer group to pray for the church. His home was open and his love was genuine. He became the focal point of much good Bible study in the congregation. His example was both genuine and contagious. To be a genuine Christian sister or brother, then, is foundational in your ministry of church renewal.

This begins where you are. It begins with you being an exhibition of the new creation and letting others get close enough to catch the contagion.

Within this context of servanthood we need to develop more specific gifts and ministries. We will look at them under four headings: (1) ministry within the Christian community or the church gathered, (2) ministry in the world as the church scattered, (3) the ministry of special callings and (4) the care and feeding of the clergy.

Ministry within the Church Gathered

Since the risen Lord has called us into his new community, his family, by the Holy Spirit, we are called to minister within that gathered community. And while we minister to our sisters and brothers, we minister primarily to God in that we bring joy to his heart. We express our love for him by loving and serving our sisters and brothers in his family. This ministry also encompasses those persons within the congregation who appear not to have a clue what the kingdom is all about, since Jesus came to seek and save them and can love them through us.

The listing of gifts and ministries in the New Testament letters (Rom 12; Eph 4; 1 Cor 12; 1 Pet 4) indicates that Jesus provides his community with what it needs to grow harmoniously into the stature of the fullness of Christ. Along with others who have written on these passages, I see these not as a complete catalog, since each list is different. Rather, they are given as "for-instances" of the way in which he may provide for his people's life and growth through such gifts and ministries as teaching, encouraging, administering, giving money or just such a practical gift as helping.

The question is natural to each of us: How do we know what

our ministry to our church family is? We do not find our ministry by going off by ourselves and deciding "my ministry is this or that." To be sure, this can happen, and such a decision can be confirmed by the community. Unfortunately, a lot of unhappy episodes have taken place when people using this procedure have not had their conclusions confirmed.

Gifts and ministries emerge in the habitat of the Spirit, which is the church. Ministry begins as life is lived in obedience to God in the church and in the world. A basic premise is that we are to be deliberately and self-consciously a servant people. We are to eschew all the human tendency toward power, prominence and control. With this understanding, gifts and ministries emerge in a natural process.

The purpose of gifts and ministries, as taught in the New Testament, is not my fulfillment but rather the encouragement and building up of the church. Unless they are exercised in genuine love, gifts are a lot of useless and noisy junk (1 Cor 13).

I see at least four obvious and principal ways in which your gifts and ministries may be called forth.

First, you might discover something that needs to be done in the congregation, or that you want to see done, and that no one else is doing. If you believe you have the capacity to do it and the congregation or its appointed leadership agrees with you, then you can assume that ministry.

Let me tell you about Heman Packard. I never met Heman Packard, since he lived before the Civil War in New Orleans. But he had been an elder in our congregation at that period and we had his diary. There is a fascinating entry that says something like this: "On this day, before the holy communion table, I vowed to God that if there was anything to be done in his church to make it fruitful, and if no one else was doing it, then I would by his grace give myself to see it done."

The renewal of the Christian church could well employ a whole order of Heman Packards! I've never met a congregation yet which did not need people like him.

Second, you might simply offer a natural talent for use among God's people. It might be anything from fixing broken johns to counseling, from teaching to keeping the nursery, from administration to fixing meals. You offer your talent to God and make it a ministry among his people.

We need to celebrate the less prominent gifts that make our life together so beautiful. Not long ago I was speaking for several nights in a church in another city. In that church is a single woman who for years has been the nursery keeper, and generations of children have their first memory of the church in her keeping. She came to speak to me after the meeting one evening and told me how glad she was that I was there, though she apologized that she hadn't heard me because she was keeping the nursery. Boy, do I ever praise God for the gift of nursery keepers!

Let me push that one a bit further. Gert Behanna amused and convicted many of us with her account of how God gave her the ministry of cleaning up the washrooms in the filling stations where she stopped for gas. I thought of Gert last fall when I stopped for a cup of coffee at a truck stop in Pennsylvania. The owner had employed a mentally handicapped young man to keep the much-trafficked men's room clean. As I went in, there was this young man lovingly polishing the urinals, obviously and with good reason proud of his work. He asked me, "Don't they look clean? Isn't the washroom nice?" It really was. I want to celebrate the guy who polished the urinals. In his work was somethin akin to the ministry of foot washing blessed by our Lord Jesus. The gift you offer to your church does not need to be a spectacular up-front ministry—there aren't many of those. It only needs to be offered to God to be used for his glory in the church.

Third, God may give you a supernatural gift or ministry. I see the gifts of tongues, healing and working of miracles in this category (1 Cor 12). These are not ordinary gifts. And you *cannot* build a strong community on these alone. But they are real and useful, and when needed the Lord blesses his people with them. They are not to be despised. If the Lord empowers you to exercise one or more of these, do it with humility and thanksgiving, but always for building up the body of Christ.

Fourth, the church may call you to exercise some gifts and ministries which you may not be aware you have. The prototype of this kind of calling would be that of Barnabas and Saul. They evidently had no notion of becoming missionaries. They were members and teachers of the new Christian community in Antioch. But as their community was gathered in fasting and prayer and seeking to be obedient, the Spirit, speaking through the community, called these two to go to a special work.

This is sometimes the congregation simply confirming a ministry which they see in you that you never recognized in yourself. I remember one evening when the couple in whose home our small group was meeting were bemoaning the fact that they weren't much good to the church since they hadn't any special gifts. In a single voice the whole group responded with the affirmation that these two had the most beautiful gift of hospitality imaginable. Their home had been a refuge for all kinds of folk and had been an encouragement to all of us. The group, then, simply confirmed and called forth a ministry which has continued to bless scores of people since then.

My recollection is that the beseiged Christian congregation in Edinburgh, Scotland, conspired to make the young John Knox their pastor and leader over his vigorous protests and unwillingness. He was to become a flaming instrument in the Lord's hand in the spiritual awakening of Scotland. Or closer to home would be an acquaintance of mine who is now teaching in a theological school. As a young engineer he was a member of a Brethren Assembly. The elders saw in him unique teaching gifts and asked him to consider going on for further biblical training with their support. He listened to them, prayed about it and concurred with the elders.

What I'm saying is that you need to be open to the Lord calling forth a gift or ministry through the voice of another or the voice of the congregation.

But be sure it is the Lord calling. If you are a willing person, and especially if you are a person of some reasonable talents, your danger is going to be that of being asked to engage in too many ministries, so many in fact that you will burn out! There is a significant difference between true gifts and ministries, and the kind of busy work and buck passing that characterizes too many congregations. Churches find a willing person and then volunteer her or him for everything that becomes available. Your own conscience needs to concur in a request from the congregation, no matter how valid. And if your heart does not respond, you need to be free to say "No, I do not believe God is leading me to engage in that work!"

At this point I can just hear someone protest that they have done all of this and it doesn't work for them, that there is no place for them to express any ministry in their church. I can hear it, and I have heard it. But wait just a minute! Even if none of what I have suggested fits you in your conscientious desire to be a church transformer, still within every church there is the need for wholesome pacesetters. There is the need for joyous and radical disciples of Jesus, the models, the paradigms and encouragers who love Jesus, who know the Scriptures, who love people, who worship, who tithe and give offerings, who invite folks in for supper, who share their Christian lives unselfishly—and in so doing bring seasons of refreshing by this ministry of incarnation.

So, don't knock it! Don't be discouraged! To be that kind of disciple is a ministry to the church gathered and makes you a gift from God to that congregation.

Ministry as the Church Scattered

The church's calling, however, is not only to be gathered, but also to be scattered as the salt of the earth and the light of the world. God's purpose is that men and women see our good works, our kingdom-shaped lives, and so glorify his name. We are called, says Peter, "to declare the praises of him who called [us] out of darkness into his wonderful light" (1 Pet 2:9 NIV).

Most of the gifts mentioned in Romans 12 and 1 Corinthians 12 are gifts to be exercised within the church as the gathered community. In the gathered community God's people come together for worship, for instruction, for prayer, for fellowship and the sharing of their lives, for equipping and for edification. But this is not to be an end in itself. Rather we come to be equipped and made ready to be sent into the world. We are gathered so that we may be scattered as an incarnation of the gospel.

Two, if not three, of the gifts mentioned in Ephesians 4:11 focus on God's saving purpose *in the world,* outside of the Christian community. An apostle is someone sent out with a commission to establish the gospel and plant churches elsewhere. This is a missionary calling. The prophetic gift can be a gift of prophetic guidance given within the church, or it can be the voice of God speaking the word of God faithfully to individuals and to structures, such as organizations, political entities, corporations and institutions outside of the church. An evangelist heralds God's thrilling news of a new order, a new aeon, a new hope that has come in the life, death and resurrection of Jesus Christ, and calls men and women to repentance and faith.

These suggest a variety of gifts given to the church scattered. There are obviously individuals especially gifted in these three areas. And because there were no clergy or professional Christians in the New Testament church, it stands to reason that such gifts were given to ordinary waiters and cooks such as Philip and Stephen (Acts 6—8). We must see that they are also part of our corporate calling and ministry to the world.

All of us have ministries both in the church gathered and in the church scattered, if we are attuned to the Holy Spirit. For some of us a primary focus will be within the gathered community as exemplified in the gift of teaching. For others the primary focus is going to be in the marketplace, in the rough and tumble of daily life outside, as the church scattered. Then we will carry out the evangelistic, prophetic and apostolic role of God's people.

Our calling to "be holy" (1 Pet 1:15) is a public calling. We are to live our lives in such a relationship of integrity with the character and will of our Father in heaven that the people and society around us will be able to discover the family likeness. Holy lives are a sign of the kingdom of God. Dietrich Bonhoeffer spells this out in a unique way in his classic *Life Together* in a chapter entitled "The Day Alone." He points out that having begun the day with the community in worship, we then go to be God's people in the world alone and in fellowship only with God. We become, in a word, the gospel in the marketplace, and this can be lonely.

This fact has been too much in eclipse. Following World War 2 there was great emphasis on the ministry of God's laity. Hendrick Kraemer wrote *The Theology of the Laity*. Hans-Ruedi Weber and others were gifted spokesmen for the ministry of the laity. Then such ministry went into an eclipse. Now Mark Gibbs is editing the Laity Exchange and re-emphasizing this ministry again.[1] All too often, however, the current emphasis on church renewal focuses on the church gathered rather than the church scattered.

A renewed Christian community is not an end in itself. The church is renewed so that the renewal, the recreation, may begin to leaven and evangelize society. We are called to minister in the marketplace, in the neighborhood, in politics and economics, in the shop, school and car pool or, in Bill Diehl's words, "in the Monday morning world."[2]

The church always faces the danger of becoming a ghe. o, becoming so focused on its own life that it forgets how to minister to the very world and to the very people whom Jesus came to seek and to save.

In the marketplace the kingdom of God encounters the kingdom of darkness. In this arena we are called to be instruments of righteousness and justice. Here God blesses the world through you and me, by demonstrating the beauty and joy of his new creation.

As you seek to know where your gifts and ministries lie, be alert to callings outside of the church community. God may be leading you to prophetic or evangelistic ministries which just may consume the major portion of your strength.

I have a friend whose professional calling is to be a motivational speaker for a large American corporation. He is sent around the country and around the world in this responsibility. As a very gifted and contagious Christian he always finds occasion in his addresses to express the power of Jesus Christ, and to do it very tactfully and pointedly. He is, then, a highly effective evangelist, and at company expense. He has warmed my heart many times telling of the aftermath of his addresses when countless persons will seek him out at happy hour or over a meal, or come to his room to find out more. The sad part of the story is that his own congregation has not been able to see this and has continually expressed its disappointment that he is not doing more busy-work in the church. Lord have mercy! They should have laid hands on him and ordained him as their evangelist to corporate America.

Perhaps we have misplaced ordination in the church. To ordain the pastor-teacher-equipper may just be putting the cart before the horse. I think of all of those I know who work hard in callings of law enforcement, public education, coffee-cup counseling and peace-making. Shouldn't their ministries be affirmed? The Christian community ought to ordain those who serve God outside in the marketplace as well as those who serve within the church gathered.

Ministry through Special Callings

Special callings are a different category. There are, and always have been, those who in acts of devotion, acts of holy recklessness, have sensed a call and have given themselves to God for service in the church, for prophetic ministries of human compassion, education or medicine—or in some creative new venture that they felt God thrusting them into. They felt that God was sending them, though no one else understood. An example of this would be St. Francis of Assisi. Francis was the popular son of a wealthy Italian merchant at a time when the flame of New Testament faith burned dim. Through several crises in his young life he sensed a call to live out a life of utter simplicity and to embody the Sermon on the Mount. He determined to become a preacher and a paradigm of the faith. Neither his family nor the church understood him. Others were drawn to him and the Franciscans became one of the most fruitful missionary movements of that period.

Then there are those whom the community thrusts out into some special work, such as Barnabas and Saul whom the church in Antioch sent out. The need for these two to go into unknown areas at the behest of the Holy Spirit was a special calling that required the rest of their lives.

Then there are those who through the mystery of God's providence find themselves in special ministries that demand their full attention. Such are persons like Chuck Colson and his prison ministry, or John Perkins and the Voice of Calvary, or Millard Fuller and Habitat for Humanity. Their involvement was not premeditated. Rather unexpected circumstances literally thrust them into these specialized ministries.

Often persons with unique skills are called to meet a special need. I think of a group of physicians from my hometown who responded to the tragic human needs in the marginalized nation of Transkei by going there to help. This happens often in our global village as those skilled in agriculture, medicine, administration and education go to meet special needs.

These callings may be long term or short term, but all of God's people, all of us, need to be open to them.

Special callings then can be very encouraging, but are not what most Christian folk are called to.

In this category go church vocations, the ordained clergy, the ministers of Word and sacrament, the priesthood, the missionary vocations, the full time or professional evangelists, and other callings of that sort. Such are not higher callings. I do not think that they are even normative. Some may not even be biblical. Yet two things must be said for such special callings: (1) in any realistic consideration of the adventure of the church, these are obviously prominent, and (2) throughout history God has chosen to use, with much blessing, many who have given themselves to him for such church vocations.

The Ministry of the Care and Feeding of the Clergy

Before we bring this adventurer's guide to a close, we need to talk about the clergy. Thus far we have been focusing on the ministry of the laity. It could be—and I say this with something between tears and laughter—that one of the most significant ministries of church renewalists might well be that of nurturing and supporting the clergy.

First, recognize that *clergy* is not even a New Testament category or designation. There appears to be no counterpart to our clergy in New Testament accounts. Yet it didn't take too many decades for clergy to make their appearance. Whether by reversion to the Old Testament pattern of priesthood, or by conforming to the pagan religions with their temple cult, or by some natural development and need for order and hierarchy, the role of the clergy appeared on the ecclesiastical stage.

Today, far too many within the church believe that if you really want to serve God in a first-class manner, then you "go into the ministry" or become clergy. Mothers and fathers aspire for their sons and daughters to become clergy as if that were especially pleasing to God. And on the wall of a theological school I visited I noticed a bronze plaque reading: "There is no higher calling in all the world than the calling to the gospel ministry." I'm sure that is affirming to the institution's students, but it reeks of clergy elitism.

One of the tragedies of this misunderstanding is that the clergy have confiscated the concept of ministry. Why else do we say, "Rev. McGregor is our minister"? The clergy has also pretty much usurped the whole notion of ordination or the laying on of hands in confirmation of a calling. Ordination is primarily focused on what we term *holy orders,* and certain functions termed *offices* of the church. Intentional or not, what this has produced is a clergy hubris, a caste of ecclesiastical Brahmins.

I say all of this, you will notice, as one of *them!*

What I want to argue here is that the New Testament focuses not on clergy but on the laity, the people of God.

To be sure, the New Testament mentions such offices as apostle, elder and bishop as well as such roles as pastoring and teaching. These roles involve brothers and sisters caring for and nurturing the flock of God. They are equippers and strategists. They are persons who give scriptural or apostolic vision and equip the people of God to minister in obedience to Christ.

Yet to focus on the clergy is to betray the true nature of the church. If the idea of clergy is to be developed from the pastor-teacher gift, then it should be an off-stage teacher-coach-model whose role is to equip the real center-stage persons, the laity, to minister day by day as Christ has called them to do.

My conviction is that the church has made a serious error here, and one that needs to be reformed. I believe that to exalt the clergy, and call them *reverend* and to make them the active, prominent and magisterial members of the Christian community unintentionally relegates the rest of the community to a more passive, secondary role whose reason for existence is to support the clergy.

But face it. Be realistic. The clergy is not going to go away. If it did go away, somebody would reinvent it. There is far too much institutional investment, too much traditional momentum, and too much influence controlled by theological seminaries in the church today to even imagine that the clergy could go into a less visible ministry.

So back to realistic church transformation. How do you affirm, encourage, minister to and hopefully recycle these brothers and sisters who happen to be clergy, and who with good intent have entered into this kind of ministry? For be well assured that such a ministry of encouragement to these clergy folk could be your most strategic and fruitful ministry of congregational transformation.

Where and how do you begin?

First off, you need to be very sensitive to them as persons. You need to recognize the unique pressures that are a part of their calling. Notice the current statistics of burn-out, divorce and personal chaos among clergy of every tradition. There are many unrealistic expectations imposed on them by the most well-meaning persons. One denominational constitution I read indicated that ordained persons have all of the gifts of the Holy Spirit and should faithfully exercise them, as well as carrying out all of those other obligations which were incumbent on all Christians. That's a heavy load to bear! Such expectations of an ordinary human being can produce defensiveness, fear, loneliness, guilt, frustration, alcoholism and chronic fatigue—especially if one is conscientious. All of these expectations are to be carried out while keeping everything in the congregation under control. What an image to maintain!

That is a worst-case description. Many clergy are ten-talent persons. Many have learned to compensate for the demands and for their own imperfections. The wise have learned escape mechanisms and created pressure valves.

But they still need ministry.

Clergy need and deserve all of those brotherly and sisterly ministries that any other member of the community needs and deserves. They need love, friendship, hospitality, affirmation and prayers. First Corinthians 16 addresses this issue. There Paul mentions all of the various kinds of caring which the church in Corinth provided for him and for Timothy. He mentions especially Stephanas, Fortunatus and Achaicus who refreshed his spirit. All pastors need some genuine, loving, warm and thoroughly human Christians around them to refresh their spirits.

In the context of such wholesome human friendship you might provide two directions of encouragement, not nagging agendas, but encouragement. First, encourage your pastors to be *real human beings*, rather than trying to live up to some artificial clergy image. Second, encourage them to be *equippers of the laity for ministry*. Help them, if they are amenable, to redefine their roles in this direction. Help them to see the dynamic and alive role of the laity.

Let them know your own need of this equipping. Help them to see the ministry of each believer in the calling of God.

I was sitting over coffee with a most creative and provocative young pastor. We were talking about this very subject, when he said, "Look, I don't want to be a Rafer Johnson in my pastoral ministry. I want to be a Bela Karolyi." When I registered incomprehension, he explained that Rafer Johnson was the superstar Olympic decathlon winner who could do everything better than anybody else. Karolyi, on the other hand, was the coach of Olympic gold medalist Mary Lou Retton. He is a big, burly, handlebar-mustachioed guy who looks as if he couldn't begin to do the gymnastics he is so good at coaching. But he knew how to teach Mary Lou Retton, and when she performed well, she ran to him and he hugged her. "So," my young friend said, "I want to teach and coach my folks to minister effectively in the world, and when they do it well, I want to hug them!" God give us more Bela Karolyi pastors, please!

I am convinced that multitudes of clergy are hungry for this kind of care and feeding. I happen to be one of those church professionals who has always had the *gift* of caring and ministering laity friends around me to keep me honest, to bear with my foibles, to encourage me in practical ways and to bless me with their love.

Any serious strategy for church renewal is going to require such a ministry to the clergy.

Conclusion

From survival in the church to redemptive ministry within the church, from an overwhelmed Shammah or a pouting Jonah to a joyous and transforming subversive—this has been our journey.

Whether you are reading this as an individual Christian, or reading it in a fellowship group, remember that the awakening of the church, the task of creating a kingdom-shaped community in your particular church, is not some illusion which you have conceived. Nor has God called you to curse the darkness or criticize the status quo. Rather he has called you to be his gift to your congregation, to be the firstfruits of his gospel in a community that will display his glory, like a crocus in the snow.

He has called you to be more than a member. He has called you to be a minister, to be a dynamic part of the mature and functioning body of Christ. And God's heart will be made glad by your obedience.

What a calling!
What a ministry!
What a God!

Epilogue

Late in the last century, the young Robert McCheyne went to be pastor of the church in the grimy industrial city of Dundee, Scotland. He was only in his midtwenties. It was a dreary city, dreary in physical appearance and dreary of soul. McCheyne prayed: "Lord, make this wilderness of chimneypots, a garden for God." By the time that McCheyne died only a few years later, that city had become the scene of one of God's gracious visitations, a veritable garden for God.

Something like McCheyne's prayer was on my mind when I prayed at the outset of writing these pages. I prayed:

Lord, make this a refreshing handbook for struggling, battle-weary, tired, run-down-at-the-heels, bored, uninspired, tradition-strangled congregations everywhere, . . . yet, where real children of God find their lot, and pray, and persevere, and serve, and hope, and listen, and stumble, and despair, and weep, and somehow find strength and communion, and You! . . . yet, knowing somehow by faith that the church is to be more than this. So anoint this book to be Your instrument. All praise to the Lamb.

I have a vision of a multitude of lovers of our Lord Jesus accepting his call to be his renewalists and to see themselves as significant evidence of a fresh, incoming tide of new life in the church around the world.

I see them, like Heman Packard, at the table of the Lord, in priestly sacrifice offering their lives for this cause and also remembering all those others who share the ministry and vision with them so that in Baptist churches in Spartanburg, or Catholic parishes in the barrios of Santiago, or Presbyterian bastions of the establishment in Pittsburgh, or quaint Episcopal churches in New England, or Bible churches in Denver, or Anglican missions in Johannesburg, there may emerge expressions of the Aeon of Life, streams of kingdom reality—love, justice, gospel, and loveliness in the midst of intensifying darkness and opposition—all flowing together in a great stream, singing the song of Moses and the Lamb, even as the hosts of darkness rally their forces in rage.

Thank you for sharing the vision with me and allowing me to walk with you through the pages of this book.

As I write this, South Africa is in bloody agony. A generation ago, Trevor Huddleston wrote from Johannesburg that in their parish of black Christians they encouraged street dances, because, he said, these black Christians were free to do what their white oppressors could not do, they could dance with joy in the streets!

May the Lord set you free to be a dancer in his church.

The irrepressible Francis of Assisi in his total love for the Savior and his uninhibited ministry of humility and servanthood and song was known as Le Jongleur de Dieu, the troubador of God.

May the Lord, by his Spirit set you free to be his troubador in the midst of the unlikely congregation where you are.

May God the Father sing for joy over you.

As an adventurer in his church may he anoint you with faith, love, hope, boldness, obedience, effective intercession and great joy . . .

> until the Spirit is poured upon us from on high,
>> and the wilderness becomes a fruitful field,
>> and the fruitful field is deemed a forest.
> Then justice will dwell in the wilderness,

and righteousness abide in the fruitful field. (Is 32:15-16
RSV)
Welcome to the adventure of the church. Welcome to the wilder-
ness which is to become God's garden!

Come Creator Spirit!

Notes

Chapter 1: Welcome to Reality
[1]As quoted in Dietrich Bonhoeffer, *Life Together* (New York: Harper and Row, 1954), pp. 17-18.

Chapter 3: The Church—Who Needs It?
[1]Ibid., pp. 77ff.
[2]Richard Lovelace, *Dynamics of Spiritual Life* (Downers Grove, Ill.: InterVarsity Press, 1979), p. 313.
[3]We use the following prayer guide at First Presbyterian Church in Hendersonville:
Prayer Ministry for First Presbyterian Church
Glorious God our Father, I spread before you these biblical concerns for the congregation. I deliberately place my own life in the middle of this prayer, asking that I may be a part of the answer. I know that these requests are made real by the Holy Spirit who "was sent" after the ascension of Jesus (1 Pet 1:12; Gal 4:6; Tit 3:6). To the eternal praise of Jesus Christ I ask:
1. that there may be created here a believing, worshiping, Spirit-filled congregation, obedient to the Great Commission, and thus a life-giving blessing to the whole body of Christ.
2. that the grace of new life in Christ may be given to all of our, as yet, unconverted members.

3. that the wholesome conviction of sin, righteousness and judgment may be given to us (Jn 16:8).

4. that the Spirit of burning may come upon our congregation to purify it and render it an obedient and holy people (Is 4:4; Mt 3:11).

5. that joy and freedom and adoration may be the hallmark of our congregational life.

6. that the spirit of love and compassion for lost and hurting and lonely men and women shall motivate us to world evangelization, turn us outward with boldness, love and imagination to find those who need to know of your love in Christ Jesus.

7. most especially that you will give to the congregation those godly, Spirit-filled leaders to lead us in the way of Christ with love and imagination. Give us laborers. Give them wisdom, understanding and insight into "the mind of the Lord" in all of the program, schedule, administration, mobilization, life, worship and outreach of the congregation that in these the Holy Spirit might reign to the glory of Christ.

8. that you will give to the congregation the attitude of generous giving that shall amply provide for our life and ministry to human need and outreach.

9. that you will graciously deal with all of those negative and Satanic elements and influences and personalities that would discourage and hinder us—that your people be not troubled.

10. that you redeem families and give special grace to single-parent families.

11. that you create among us a soul-thirst for yourself, a hungering and thirsting for the things of God.

12. that you will anoint and bless all of those who minister among us as teachers, encouragers, choir members, action group workers, pastors, intercessors and church staff. Be present to nurture and prosper our ministry to youth and children, to each other, to the hurting and broken, and to the community around us.

Lord God, I come to you in the company of many others in the congregation to pray that for the praise of your own name you will create here a "flaming fellowship" in yourself. Be so real and adored among us that in the midst of the darkness we may shine as lights to your everlasting praise. Do a new thing among us. Make me—and us—to be disciples of Jesus Christ who can then make disciples of others. Create a sensitive, interdependent, supportive fellowship in the Holy Spirit. Help us to "walk the talk" and be so contagious that others will be attracted irresistibly to Jesus Christ. Make us to be instruments of justice and peace.

Thank you that all of these requests are things you have encouraged us to pray and so we have confidence that we are praying in your will.

All praise to the Lamb of God! Hallelujah! Amen.

Chapter 4: Do-It-Yourself Disciplemaking

[1]Eugene Peterson, *A Long Obedience in the Same Direction* (Downers Grove, Ill.:

InterVarsity Press, 1980).

²John R. W. Stott, *Basic Christianity* (Downers Grove, Ill.: InterVarsity Press, 1958).

³Dietrich Bonhoeffer, *The Cost of Discipleship* (New York: The Macmillan Co., 1948).

⁴Reuben P. Job and Norman Shawchuck, *A Guide to Prayer for Ministers and Other Servants* (Nashville: The Upper Room, 1983).

⁵Segundo Galilea, *Following Jesus* (Maryknoll, N.Y.: Orbis, 1981) and *The Beatitudes: To Evangelize as Jesus Did* (Maryknoll, N.Y.: Orbis, 1984).

⁶John White, *The Fight* (Downers Grove, Ill.: InterVarsity Press, 1976); Calvin Miller, *The Singer, The Song, The Finale* (Downers Grove, Ill.: InterVarsity Press, 1975, 1977, 1979).

⁷Their address is Scripture Union, 1716 Spruce Street, Philadelphia, PA 19103.

⁸R. C. Sproul, *Knowing Scripture* (Downers Grove, Ill.: InterVarsity Press, 1977); Gordon D. Fee and Douglas Stuart, *How to Study the Bible for All Its Worth* (Grand Rapids, Mich.: Zondervan, 1982).

⁹John Bright, *The Kingdom of God* (Nashville: Abingdon Press, 1953); Robert T. Henderson, *Joy to the World* (Atlanta: John Knox Press, 1980); Donald B. Kraybill, *The Upside Down Kingdom* (Scottdale, Penn.: Herald Press, 1978); Mortimer Arias, *Announcing the Reign of God* (Philadelphia, Penn.: Fortress Press, 1984).

¹⁰Martin E. Marty, *A Short History of Christianity* (New York: Fontana Books, 1959).

¹¹J. I. Packer, *Knowing God* (Downers Grove, Ill.: InterVarsity Press, 1973).

¹²Rebecca Manley Pippert, *Out of the Saltshaker* (Downers Grove, Ill.: InterVarsity Press, 1979).

¹³Willian E. Diehl, *Thank God It's Monday* (Philadelphia: Fortress Press, 1982); Richard J. Mouw, *Called to Holy Worldliness* (Philadelphia: Fortress Press, 1980).

¹⁴Alfred C. Krass, *Evangelizing Neopagan North America* (Scottdale, Penn.: Herald Press, 1982). This book is valuable because of its incisive critique of the North American culture and church. The brief section of the homophilia-homophobia ethical question is, however, enigmatic.

¹⁵David Bryant, *In the Gap: What It Means to Be a World Christian* (Ventura, Calif.: Regal Books, 1984).

¹⁶Bonhoeffer, *Cost of Discipleship.*

¹⁷Howard A. Snyder, *The Community of the King* (Downers Grove, Ill.: InterVarsity Press, 1977).

¹⁸David Augsburger, *Caring Enough to Confront* (Ventura, Calif.: Regal Books, 1973); Em Griffin, *Getting Together: A Guide to Good Groups* (Downers Grove, Ill.: InterVarsity Press, 1982).

¹⁹Lovelace, *Dynamics of Spiritual Life.*

Chapter 5: Toward a Kingdom-shaped Community

¹Ray C. Stedman, *Body Life* (Glendale, Calif.: Regal Books, 1972).

²Herman Ridderbos, *The Coming of the Kingdom* (Philadelphia: The Presbyterian and Reformed Publishing Co., 1962), p. 354. This scholarly treatise has been one of the single most catalytic influences in my own Christian thought.

Chapter 6: Redemptive Subversion: Prayer & Faith

[1]I am altogether indebted to Charles Davis who opened my eyes to the faith, love and hope themes and their relevance to church renewal in his *A Question of Conscience* (New York: Harper and Row, 1967).

Chapter 7: Redemptive Subversion: Love & Hope

[1]I am indebted for this liberating theme to Jacques Ellul, *Ethics of Freedom* (Grand Rapids, Mich.: Eerdmans, 1976).

[2]Davis, *Question of Conscience,* p. 110.

[3]P. T. Forsyth, *The Soul of Prayer* (London: Independent Press, 1916), p. 12.

Chapter 8: Beyond Membership to Ministry

[1]Laity Exchange Books (Fortress Press) is a whole series under the editorship of Mark Gibbs focusing on dimensions of the ministry of the laity. The books by Diehl and Mouw mentioned earlier are part of this series.

[2]Diehl, *Thank God It's Monday.*